UNDISCOVERED PALADINS

also by j.d.tulloch

Neutral Receding Lines: Road Rhymes, Volume Two

Hypnotizing Lines: Road Rhymes, Volume One

The Will to Resist: And Psalms of Anger, Love & Humanity

edited by j.d.tulloch

Desolate Country: We the Poets, United, Against Trump

Prompts! A Spontaneous Anthology

UNDISCOVERED PALADINS
WESTWARD RHYMES REVISITED

J.D. TULLOCH

39 WEST PRESS

39 WEST PRESS
Kansas City, MO
www.39WestPress.com

Copyright © 2015 by j.d.tulloch

All rights reserved.

No part of this book may be reproduced, scanned, or distributed in any printed or electronic form, including information storage and retrieval systems, without permission. Please do not participate in or encourage piracy of copyrighted materials in violation of the author's rights.

Please purchase only authorized editions.

First Edition: October 2015

ISBN: 978-0-9908649-1-2

Library of Congress Control Number: 2015915015

This book is a work of fiction. Names, characters, places, dates, and incidents are products of the author's imagination, or are used fictitiously, satirically, or as parody. Any resemblance to actual persons, living or dead, business establishments, events, or locales is entirely coincidental.

10 9 8 7 6 5 4 3

Book Design & Layout: j.d.tulloch

39WP-09

"I have crossed seas, left cities behind me,
followed the course of rivers or plunged into forests,
always making my way towards other cities ...
And all that led *me—where*?"

Jean-Paul Sartre
Nausea (1938)

CONTENTS

Prologue xi

ROUTE ONE: A GEST WEST

Hypnotized	3
Jesus & the Church of Malt Liquor	6
Progression in G(A) Minor	7
Wine & Semen	8
Ostensibly: Ogden	9
Wired	10
At Last	12
Lasciate ogne speranza, voi ch'intrate	14
Mephistopheles, the Hustler & a Gyro	15
(Properly) Not a Poem	16
Sunday in Portland OR: Sue Me George Lucas	17
Petrified: A TriMet Adieu	18
Up to Whom?	19
Circuit Board Blues	20
Again	22
Keep Right	23
Pleeeeeethora	24
Big Tree	25
Five Haiku	26
Missing the Beat	27
Big Little Reno	31
Yosemite	32
My Turn (Abridged)	33

ROUTE TWO: LAS VEGAS AWAKE

Paradise (Next	37
Las Vegas Awake	38
Dream to Sleep	40
Valleys of Fire	41
Beating Las Vegas	43
Starving	44
The Feast	45
Leftovers	46
The Discarded Queen	47
Bad Music	48
Oh No (The Second Coming)	49
Heart of the Coconut: The Faux Colossus	50
HOT SEXY GIRLS	51
Govern or? (The Con of Sin)	54
Noodled	56
A Lonely Haiku	57
Lost City	58
Neon Roses	60
Chasing Ghosts	62
Burning Ocean	64
Somewhere	66
Melody #87	67
He Ain't Heavy; He's My Brother	69
Body Bags	72
Dizzy Math (The Thizz of Nature)	73
The ~~Myth~~ Meth of Change	74
A New Day	75
Las Vegas Awake (Reprise)	76
Racing Nowhere	77

ROUTE THREE: HOLLYWOOD ALLURE

Pilot Season	81
Soon Wilshire Soon	83
Past Palisades Park	85

LOS ANGELES OUTLOOK	86
WANNABES	87
HOLLYWOOD ALLURE	89
A HOLLYWOOD RHYME	90
MEANWHILE, I-($%#@&)	91
STARS IN THE BACKGROUND	92
BEVERLY CENTER: EMPTY—	94
A NARCISSIST ON SANTA MONICA BEACH	95
THEY	96
MEET ME	97
DIRTY DIRTY ECHO PARK	98
SOMNOLENT STARS	99
DB ON THE THIRD STREET PROMENADE	100
BERNIE THE HOMELESS GUY	102
L.A. BREAKFAST WITH A PROFESSOR EMERITUS	103
A SCENE AT GRIFFITH PARK	104
MIRRORED SUNSET	105
PILOT SEASON (REPRISE)	106
CONTENTIOUS CLOUDS	107

ROUTE FOUR: BACKSTREET MARGINALIA

PRNDL: TRANSMISSION	111
RHYMES OF ANCIENT MARINERS	112
OCEAN BEACH	114
HOUNDS OF HELL	116
LOG CABIN LAMENT	117
SUPERSTITION AIN'T THE WAY	118
DARK AGES	119
THE TRUTH (FROM A HOTEL ROOM IN FLAGSTAFF)	120
BECOMING	121
A TRUCK STOP IN RED ROCK, NEW MEXICO	123
CHECK YOUR SIX	125
)E-M-O-H(	127
DING-DONG! THE DICK IS DEAD	128
LONESOME LANGSTON	129
GUNPOWDERVODKACOWSHIT	130

Café Ephemera	131
Goodbye	133
Burning Jazz	134
Giant Steps	135
Taming Lions	136
Vanishing	137
Snowflakes	138
Innocence: Gone	139
)e-m-o-H(too: Sleepless Blues	140
Hiatus: of	141
The Beat of Beats Passed	145
PRNDL: Anamnesis	146

PROLOGUE

SHE IS AS GOOD as new and ready to hit the road on what might be her final curtain call: one last gest—a cross-country pilgrimage—to both lands unseen and destinations revisited. *The Lincoln* (my reliable traveling companion), restored within the confines of a limited budget and (*mostly*) reborn to her original 1997 glory, embarked with me on what now has evolved into a fifty-thousand-plus mile journey of self-exploration and discovery, seeking not necessarily more fruitful pastures but rather trekking westward—and then eastward—on a noble quest of inspiration, an escapade of adventure, in search of an American Dream that once hearkened the spirits of forgotten voyagers who beckoned me from afar as Horace Greeley loudly whispered in my ear, "Go west, young man ... Go west."

◆

BLANK STARES POPULATE THE faces of what Emory University English Professor and Donald J. Trump supporter Mark Bauerlein dubs "The Dumbest Generation," the fifty million "diverted, distracted, and devoured" minds of Millennials and Echo Boomers who represent Generation Y, The Google Generation, or Gen Net.

But Bauerlein's labeling of only Millennials as "The Dumbest Generation" expresses a short-sided world view and a misplaced condemnation of only a small percentage of the over two billion global adherents of the Facebook Fad, a peer-pressure driven social networking culture of assimilation that distracts users from the realities of the world—by repeatedly trending "news" stories that are actually works of fiction while simultaneously capitalizing on an advertising policy that permits politicians to lie on its platform—and focuses their attentions on interpersonal social dramas, which devour thoughts with unnecessary obsessions that entirely revolve around knowing exactly what online "friends" are up to (and thinking about) each minute of the day.

"The Dumbest Generation" should be defined more accurately to include all passive participants of *The Information Age*: the majority of Web users who access the Internet only to consume commercial media, which includes both *news* and entertainment, and/or engage in the *creation* and exchange of typical (and chiefly humdrum) user-generated content (memes, selfies, status updates, unnuanced commentary, etc.) via social media, representing, therefore, a trans-generational phenomenon—aptly referred to here as *The Borg Generation* (apologetically borrowed from the *Star Trek* antagonist comprised of a hive of assimilated drones)—where citizens of all ages plug into a global collective of electronic voyeurism and narcissism that employs auto-paparazzo and self-adulation—and whose major purpose, in essence, is to project to others an overly aggrandized and well-crafted façade, a bleached (yet revealing) narrative, of one's own ego-centric perception of themselves (their "likes," their individuality, their political and religious views, their social standing and self-professed importance in the world, etc.)—by way of status updates, wall posts, ~~six-second looping "vines,"~~ lip-synced "TikToks," ephemeral "snaps," filtered faux-Polaroid "insta" images, and two hundred eighty character "tweets," creating slangs of reduced vocabulary while eliminating complex thought, abolishing insightful reflection, and reducing articulate prose to the lowest common denominator, forever trapping the majority of partakers in a prison of postponed social, emotional, and cerebral development.

While information is more readily available to The Borg Generation than to any previous generation following the advent of writing in the fourth millennium BCE, the sources of this instantaneous information emanate from fewer and fewer providers (Google Search, Facebook News Feeds, Twitter Timelines, etc.), and the contents of the bulk of information *discovered* online are determined solely by proprietary algorithms that aggregate previously collected personal data, thus limiting online users' exposures to viewpoints differing from their own while activating them in a manner that elicits an emotional reaction, accentuates extremism, and subjects them to intrusive, behavioral-tracking commercial advertisements designed to embolden superfluous consumerism, by changing how we think about ourselves, in a brazen attempt to convince us of what we *want* and/or like well before we even know what it is that we actually *need*.

Furthermore, compelling evidence suggests that big data billionaire Robert Mercer—in concert with his now defunct data-analytics firm Cambridge Analytica, which for political advertising purposes illegally harvested the personal data of millions of Facebook users without their consent—is at the heart of a multimillion-dollar propaganda network designed to attack the credibility of the centrist media and supplant it with questionable right-wing sites, such as Breitbart, which he co-owns. In the same agitprop vein, Google's search ranking system is being "manipulated and controlled" by tech-savvy radical right-wing groups—what the media has dubbed the "alt-right," a deceptively benign phrase used to rebrand and downplay the intolerant and fundamentally racist beliefs of white supremacists (neo-Nazis)— with their hate sites dominating the results of basic keyword searches on Muslims, Jews, Hitler, and women, thus emboldening a once fringe movement that also has been energized, wrongly validated, and elevated into the mainstream by the dangerous ideologies of key White House advisers and the inflammatory statements and puerile tweets of demagogue and narcissist-in-chief Trump, who intentionally diffuses bigotry, misogyny, homophobia, Islamophobia, and anti-Semitism into the norm of propaganda already present within the misinformation bubble of most people's mediacentric lives.

As a direct result of the lack of ethics behind the questionable business practices and supercilious rhetoric of the aforementioned information monopolies and data-analytics firms, more and more "prisoners" *willfully* sit shackled in the darkness of Plato's cave (*The Republic: Book VII*) and consequently remain unenlightened concerning basic scientific, political, and historical facts. The majority of social media users, in truth, fail to comprehend the simple tenet behind the massive revenue generation and vast market caps of data mining firms such as Facebook and Google—that they, the users of "free" Internet *services*, are not the customers of these companies; they are these companies' uncompensated products, target demographics, who unknowingly pay a great price for the catered (and often narrow in scope) information they seek: the commodification of personal data and the elimination of privacy.

Therefore, within this maelstrom of technological modernity—where we stand (perpetually) at the edge of an intellectual, cultural, and (potentially catastrophic) global economic crisis—the real test of our survival and continued evolution as a cognizant people hinges on our concerted efforts to vet and validate information—especially content emanating from traditionally unreliable sources—before sharing it with others and virally broadcasting it across cyberspace, to remain skeptical of unsubstantiated claims that contradict all aspects of higher reasoning, and to resist blanket surrender of our valuable, personal data to what (on the surface) appear to be trustworthy online corporate entities: cleverly designed colorful logos camouflaging hidden server farms that hover magically in the "cloud" of data control. Instead, we must pool our resources (and talents) and put the full puissance of our labors into developing—independent of privacy-invading, data-collecting, information-disseminating *platform* corporations—innovative (and open sourced) methods of securely accessing, absorbing, and circulating accurate and constructive information via the au courant technological might that sits freely at our disposal.

In the mid-fifteenth century, those in power saw Guttenberg's movable type printing press and subsequent distribution of one hundred eighty Bibles as the potential bastion of downfall of elite control over the masses—knowledge is power. In many ways, that new medium of communicating information on a broader scale facilitated the mainstreaming—not commercialization—of counter-culture and allowed novel ideas that contradicted archaic thought to spread amongst the multitudes, thereby propelling a Renaissance of science, art, and literacy.

To many people, however, the printing press seems outdated by today's technological standards. With a computer—or smart phone—and an Internet connection, any global citizen has the potential to reach far more *blank* minds than Guttenberg's Bible ever did. The Internet, accessed through applications and the World Wide Web, garnishes the capacity to invoke positive changes that benefit all of humanity—as we have seen in the social-media-led Arab Spring revolutions in Tunisia, Libya, Yemen, and Egypt—not just app developers, Silicon Valley, and Wall Street.

Even after Edward Snowden's damning (and frightening) revelations of the NSA's unconstitutional global spying programs, which, unfortunately, have had little effect on people's cyberspace habits (save the decline in searches of NSA watchwords), the potential, and yet mostly unharnessed, power of online activism remains awesome. But at the same time, by virtue of Internet and social networking companies' earnings goals and indubitable attempts to appease shareholders by connecting and monetizing the usernames, MAC addresses, IP addresses, IMEI numbers, advertising/cookie IDs, GPS locations, etc. of anyone who goes online, distraction—as a consequence of the unbridled accumulation, manipulation, and self-dissemination of personal data—runs amok on the Net, latently creating false realities by promoting the propagation of fake news and hate speech via data science and bot armies, the incessant barrage of lies and disinformation spewed by our elected officials, the proliferation of targeted advertising based on multi-platform behavioral tracking, and the promulgation of worthless information (e.g., when your co-worker last had a bowel movement) regurgitated by our "friends," thereupon wantonly deflecting us from the worthwhile information that actually affects the quality of our daily lives as well as our economic well-being.

◆

WHILE SIPPING LUKEWARM COFFEE in a sterile, Internet café and reflecting upon where my travels with *The Lincoln* have led me (which included stops at the now failed #OccupyWallStreet movements of New York, Chicago, Kansas City, Seattle, Portland, San Francisco, Los Angles, Las Vegas, Minneapolis, Madison, and others), it would be presumptuous to assume that a *printed* book of road musings masquerading as poems qualifies as worthwhile information, but I do, however, hope my words from the road arouse the contagion of inspiration in the hearts and minds of in-the-know artists, actors, and activists; singers, songwriters, and musicians; painters, filmmakers, and writers; and independent entrepreneurs and business owners who, through simply saying "no," choose to transcend the control of mainstream corporate, capitalist ideology and instead strive to create a self-realized American Dream of know how vis-à-vis self-explorative creative, artistic, and transparent commercial endeavors that selflessly serve to uplift the majority of humanity rather than further facilitating the advancement and concentration of wealth of the minority of individuals and immortal corporations who economically enslave us all.

We must stand together, and apart, in unison and discord, as a generation of knowing individuals whose ideas and ideals aim to focus our collective energies on social change rather than social networking, on tearing down walls rather than (building or) posting gossip to them, and on fostering face to face connections rather than facebooking from afar, thus sowing the seeds of a twenty-first century renaissance where each individual embraces an empathetic existential freedom and embarks on a voyage of self-discovery that immediately seizes life and unselfishly makes the most of each opportunity by putting the shared needs of humankind first and the self-centered desires of the individual last. Our survival depends upon it. *Welcome to the k(no)w ...*

ROUTE ONE
A GEST WEST

HYPNOTIZED

      Rolling—
Kansas Flint Hills
Natural prairie land
Of majesty tenders endless
Puissance, supply: windmill farms
Arising from the abyss of eternity
Prodigious pallid turbines litter
The landscape surrenders
To the (green) generation
Of clean renewable energy
Courtesy the territory's
Power-providing monopoly.

      Hypnotizing lines repeat continuously,
      mile after mile, guiding travel.

      Broadcasting—
Thermometer's sturdy
102 yields not
The cabin of *The Lincoln* survives
A sanguine struggle to keep cool
Food and fuel anticipate
Hays' relocated Rome
Buffalo roam
Bill Cody's defunct
Cholera-plagued home
On the range
Now estranged
From home
The Home
I no longer
Know a thirst to
Exchange Midwest heat for
Sweet mountain breeze.

       Billowing—
Boulder's streets dominate
Rockies' reflection
At sunset red glare
Interstate-70 wears
Heavy splattered insects litter
The windshield buries
Minute life succumbing
Tragically seared by
A slab of safety glass soaring
Through anonymous air
Caskets at seventy-two.

       Hypnotizing lines repeat, continuously,
       mile after mile, guiding arrival.

       Riding—
Cyclists bank on
Bike lanes running
Parallel city roads proffer
Parking racks galore evoke
Berkeley East

(Green) eco
Friendly buses burn
Clean diesel transports
Scores down town
Pedestrian traffic dominates
Street theatre prevails.

LEFT: Slow-motion mimes chase imaginary poisonous arrows like Cupid trying to reclaim a misfire, an ill-conceived match destined for failure.

RIGHT: Sleight of hand magicians deceive onlookers, momentarily sidetracking shoppers searching for sizzling sales at trendy boutiques.

FRONT: A juggler twirls sticks of fire, a sideshow distraction to a musician magically plucking his semi-acoustic guitar in unison with a stale carnival keyboard.

BACK: An out of place suit screams out the disastrous details of his tee time tomorrow, insisting that his voice be heard above the rest.

SIDE: A non-metered sprinter swiftly passes by carrying a forlorn fare piggy-back style.

OUT: I am surrounded alone

                (unseen)

       Hypnotizing lines repeat continuously,
       mile after mile, beckoning sweet mountain breeze
       guiding me down the street.

Jesus & the Church of Malt Liquor

a trinity of dirty hippies
    (with nothing but a bongo)
        mistakes my
            rolled fag
                for a spliff.

a congregation of thirty tourists
    (with nothing but green)
        mistakes the
            paroled stags
                for riffraff.

de jesus of sturdy boulder
    (with nothing but *songo*)
        mistakes his)
            $(old scags
                for a fatted calf.

a tea party of quirky white-breads
    (with nothing but sheen)
        mistakes their
            gold bags
                for the staff of life.

a dirty hippie was Jesus & The Church of Malt Liquor
now accepts donations, change with a promise:
collections purchase nothing but booze: salvation.

Progression in G(A) Minor

befogged by daybreak's dawn like a fawn confronting
first light upon deserting her mother's womb, the
asphalt amuses as if the Colorado State Police were

on my t(r)ail. the Wyoming line could not sooner
consummate my relationship with US-287, but Fort
Collins' sprawl slows my descent to a rapid crawl.

caffeine dreams' wired nightmares mar patience—
delayed, like a refugee seeking safe access through
over around under The *Great* Mexican Wall, only to

be held by an after-market governor restricting
Time's precarious passage. at last, unmolested
advance, but Laramie re-sounds Matthew Shepard's

closeted cry. like a ghostly mist i flee silent
symphonies carelessly composed by hayseed
sociopaths and advance on a path where broken

mountains marry hodgepodge plains' crescendoing
plateaus with out objection from traditional foes.
faraway from somewhere (nowhere better explains),

i survive
as the conveys of slower soldiers to my right
expire in the night.

i progress
as the solitary soldier
is martyred in the night.

Wine & Semen

from the rostrum of the Gothic temple
the quorum of twelve (balding men)
disciples its white bread wisdom

to gullible followers

disappeared golden tablets reappear
in a book believed only by a Moron(i):
Chapter 5 declares Joseph Smith savors

wine

swapped for water by explicative elders:
the shed blood of Christ the Savior
circulates crystal clear in holy sacrament's

prohibition

saves sobriety in the land of holy misogyny:
women worship as nothing more than
childbearing vassals, vessels for Mormon

semen

left behind on crusty fast food napkins:
loads self-anointed by homefree hippies
shuffling (one last time) down secular

Salt Lake streets

coerce the budding exodus of disembodied
dilettantes leading leafless drum circles
back to baked Boulder for the summer

Ostensibly: Ogden

      i'm told
      Two-Bit Street
      was too seedy for
      Al Capone:

illicit street gambling walking narcotics bootleggers trafficking
refuge supplied by
speakeasies
safe Sanctuary

      i'm told
      Two-Bit Street
      was tamed by
      Mormons:

twenty till ten tattoo parlor padlocked Tabernacle trafficking
refuge supplied by
a single saloon
speak-easing
soloed songs slamming
abuse cantos of latter day obsessions emitting
patchoulied sounds indistinct odors reeking
staled cigars resonating
proverbial open-miked coffee shops pinching
joseph smith's wives re-birthing
the guarantee of
safe sanctuary

      i'm told
      Two-Bit Street
      was too seedy for
      Al Capone:

secure Alcatraz isle
supplies
safer Sanctuary

WIRED

                halfway
to the North Pole
mainlined adrenaline courses
coasting veins downward
      effortlessly
            descending
                    the 45th parallel

injecting six degree declines
build momentum
      gallantly
           sailing

at extraneous speeds of
eighty p
      l
     u
    m
     m
      e
       t
       i
        n
        g
like eight Mark VIII torpedoes
h u n t i n g targets unseen

      swiftly
streets akin
to Nice
present delusions
of formula one
submersibles racing
                p u m p i n g

popping ears
compress
      c o m p e t i n g
          to sustain sea-lagged cylinders

Idaho sinks sunset
Oregon cascades
hazard lights ahead of
green forest air inhaled in
synonymous breaths with
fresh Danish shag

waiting submissively
      (wasting)
as the slug impeding procession
creeps onward in the rayless
dimness of dominate dusk

waiting aggressively
      (basting)
as Portland's radiance
emerges from the ray less
dominance of dusk

At Last

Skidmore fountain reflects skid row: a one-armed vagabond serves the soundtrack for the day's festivities, painting abstract portraits of Willie Nelson while delicately strumming banging flat-picking raping caressing the neck of his jaded guitar with a splayed wooden stick deftly affixed to the nub of his right arm.

A dollar bill escapes my front pocket and easily squats shelter in his tip jar—an upside-down ten-gallon Stetson—summoning a later cause for celebration as discovery of my ~~generosity~~ blunder sends him twenty reasons to continue entertaining.

Not wanting to be upstaged, a pewter statue dances to life and slowly shifts from stoic Moses to dying Gaul, startling a small child, unaware that the sham stone sculpture stinks charlatan: an out-of-work actor layered with pounds of silver make-up in perfect disguise.

Twin glass towers mount whiskey river banks, ripping currents through the Saturday market that resemble the sounds of shells firing from an AK-47, but no need for panic as a German tourist sporting a brand-new SLR camera is spotted snapping hundreds of shots of his six-year-old daughter in a split-second.

Cosseted under the shade of an English elm, a dread-locked hippie sits sketching a charcoal drawing of the homeless man sleeping silently on the fading lawn in front of him, both ignorant of adjacent tent city's bustling peddler's paradise populated by active artists hocking hand-crafted wares: merchandise manufactured and marketed with the hope of maintaining a bohemian lifestyle.

With a heaping plate of Himalayan in hand, West Wind
   wrestles the water below and whips the promenade
   repeatedly, rhythmically fashioning a soothing zephyr that
   wafts the halfzware shag from my hemp paper, percolating the
   implausibility of rolling the perfect smoke or consuming curry
   dumplings lentils rice green beans potatoes tomatoes
   cucumbers in blissful ardor.

But—
   My hunger pains wait.
   My nicotine fix waits.

From its unselfish flowing fountain,
   surfeited skid row serves something recycled:
   a serendipitous slice of self-determination.

Ingesting my own sovereignty
   I am.

   I am (free)
   at last.

Lasciate ogne speranza, voi ch'intrate.

Downtown Portland bustles pedestrian passengers:
    colonies of army ants
    vacating the district
    for asylum in suburban
    hills after collecting
    daily supplies
    of pests
    from *en masse*
    column raids.

City Center spits out a mob of migrant middlemen:
    swarms of worker bees
    fleeing the urban core
    for asylum in suburban
    hives after collecting
    daily supplies
    of pollen
    from flowering
    office cubicles.

Dusk dawns a nocturnal crew of culture's underbelly:
    canvassing clans of homeless hippies
    (with pan flutes and bongo drums)
    staking claims
    to urban street corners
    and panhandling for currency
    like Pavlovian puppies
    pleading for treats
    from enabling masters.

Oh Virgil! Guide me through this fiery Inferno.
    Protect me from Geryon's treachery and deceit.
    And I promise not to ditch you in Purgatorio.

Mephistopheles, the Hustler & a Gyro

Mephistopheles traps me at the bar
   While sipping Goldschläger from a snifter,
   And thus commences our shibboleth spar.

Assuming I'm nothing but a drifter,
   The ponytailed shrink starts his assessment;
   So, I swiftly don the role of grifter.

A two-buck beer his lofty investment,
   But his rhapsodic rants fail to amuse
   As does his plea for my shirt's divestment.

Loaded with piety and full of booze,
   I flee Silverado for the dank street
   In search of a surrogate muse to schmooze.

On the concrete looms impending repeat:
   A sobbing hustler swapping sex bizarre.
   I hastily flee his web of deceit,

   But he pursues me to the dining car.
   I gift a gyro and say *au revoir*.

(Properly) Not a Poem

Friends engage in mass Diaspora,
spreading themselves thin
across the land like
earth's inhabitants
after Babel's
fall.

Instagram Facebook Twitter texts Four-Square connects.

Letters
lost smiling
at strangers on
sidewalk trash littering
street curb transgressions
denying forgiveness bottled zones
comforting perspiration bonging fast
food seeking guitar bass trumpets contagion.

Inspiration.

(Properly)

future

Sunday in Portland OR: Sue Me George Lucas

Beyoncé, Sweetie Pie,
and the slightly evil Bugsy
   (innocently)
peck at my feet

Anakin
   (patiently)
mans the flames
of the barbecue

Princess Leia
   (reluctantly)
remains skeptical
of her inflatable pool

Queen Amidala
   (diligently)
searches the backyard
for freshly laid chicken eggs

Has heaven reared its ugly head?
NO—

Portland Sunday
   (intentionally)
sows the seeds
of trademark infringement

OR:
Sue me George Lucas*

---

*On 30 October 2012, The Walt Disney Company agreed to acquire Lucasfilm Ltd. from George Lucas for $4.05 billion, half in cash plus 40 million Disney shares, making Lucas the second largest non-institutional shareholder of Disney, behind the trust of the late Steve Jobs. Lucas has pledged "to donate the majority of the proceeds to his philanthropic endeavors."

Petrified: A TriMet Adieu

the libidinous blonde
decorates the aisle

with a short skirt
fresh off the rack.

she sits next to me.

her ringless finger
(and dreaded hair)

shimmers sunlight
beaming through

cabin's portal,
recalling Medusa.

petrified, i revisit Foucault and *Folie et déraison*
while she studies magic bras in *Glamour*.

i suspect we have little in common.

Up to Whom?

With help seizing the night
It seemed (at the time)

A good idea drinking
A bottle of generic NiteTime.

Under the influenza of
Self-induced twilight dreams …

Reality floated by my bed room depot
Without a seat to spare.

Under the influenza of
Self-induced twilight dreams …

Fantasy floated by my bed room depot
With some change to spare.

Tomorrow?
Up to me. Up to you. Up to us.

Circuit Board Blues

Echo's forlorn cries ricochet from the glens,
        prophetically project soothing sounds
        through the æther that reverberate in
        the depths of consciousness, reflect the
        almighty authority of the ocean, and
        surreptitiously summon me to the sea.

Portland daytrippers maraud along the highway
        in hybrid chariots and descend like
        medieval Norse Vikings invading Cannon
        Beach's reticent settlement, pilfering
        every dry dock within beach's reach.

Low lying clouds imitate the colour of The Deep
        and merge with the horizon, fusing sky's
        end and the beginning of Poseidon's realm.

Haystack Rock and her twin needled companions
        protrude from the brine and remind me
        where my self-imposed banishment began
        miles down beach's end.

High tide delivers a solitary surfer who catches
        a right and cross-steps down the deck of
        his longboard before needlessly grubbing.

A pending tempest produces no magnificent sunset
        today, but the fresh fragrance of the ocean
        wind sends chills down my spine as my spirit
        skyrockets over my body into the clouds
        above and back down to the waves below.

Instantly—
        all thoughts flee my head in a meditative
        state of holy supreme euphoric dystopia.

Momentarily—
> I stop breathing (and my heart ceases
> beating) while duality direct dials me
> into the circuit board's broadband modem
> of universal connectivity.

Simultaneously—
> I am
> snorkeling the coral reefs of the Great Guana Cay
> sculling the quick waters of the muddy Missouri
> sinking into the snow white sands of Pensacola Beach
> motoring a nameless lake after pirating a clipper
> commuting by express boat down the Chao Phraya
> skiffing in the Gulf of Mexico outside New Orleans
> surfing Ocean Beach breakers right of the jetty
> captaining a sailboat in a regatta in Mobile Bay
> arriving via schooner into Victoria Harbour at sunset.

Tragically—
> I am
> satisfied
> > content
> > > at peace

Eternally—
> I am
> you
> > (are me)
> > > we are
> > > > here

> > > > > I wish
> > > > > you
> > > > > were
> > > > > here.

Again

Juliet said to Romeo:
"Parting is such sweet sorrow."

But de-parting Portland
and venturing down
the California coast
I refuse to say ~~goodbye~~
              adiós to my friends.

Goodbye exists for eternity—
like writing your name
in freshly poured concrete:
immortalized for perpetuity
on the Grecian Urn of Time
for all of humanity to see.

Instead—
I ephemerally inscribe
UNTIL WE MEET AGAIN
on the wet sands
of a beach
somewhere near
Crescent City.

By the time
the fleeting tide
crashes ashore
and washes away
the sentiment,
I will have returned
from the sea
to see
you
again.

Keep Right

California road signs exclaim:
    SLOWER TRAFFIC KEEP RIGHT

Oregonian drivers tread
into California proceed
ignorant to advice carry on
refuse to yield to faster vehicles

Portland's political correctness amok proclaims:
    DO NOT PUMP PETROL
    DO NOT PICK UP PILGRIM PASSENGERS
    DO NOT PONTIFICATE ON A PHONE WHILE POUNDING THE PAVEMENT
    PLEASE POSSESS POT FOR PERSONAL PUTREFACTION

Cosmos whispers to searching shepherds:
    tap high a dormant keg
    awake like Goldilocks a hibernating bear

                                          (redemption)

    spawn common courtesy
    shun selfish deeds
    seamlessly merge into the alliance of awareness

        &

altruistically allow those
on/in a different (p)lane
to pass freely into obscurity

Pleeeeeethora

SOUTH
down *The 101*

ODYSSEY
into Humboldt County

primordial ooze
impregnates my quintessence

the smell of KB
loads my lungs
with unsullied ocean ozone
filling them to capacity
like ignited propane gas
expelling super-heated air
inflating the envelope
of a hot air balloon

moments before
its thin epidermal layer RU P T U R E S
i relax

the sensation
sweeps through my soul
like the morning dew
passing through
the canopy of
any
RED
wood
park
randomly discovered
by the mapping service
of a popular Internet
~~search engine~~ data miner

Big Tree

timeless trees scrape the skyline,
shading squadrons of safarists
from scintillating summer sun.

Big Tree audaciously ascends from
California soil into the stratosphere,
invading Zeus' sphere of influence

and angering him enough to send
clear-cutters to the realm below,
punishing the titanic trees for hubris.

but Gaia intervenes, saving
the redwood groves for her
enervated earth children.

rings later—

regal redwoods assume their rightful
thrones with divine right proudly project
wisdom's power to their forest subjects.

it's safe out here, secluded from
the city (protected from the
elements) by my redwood rulers.

it's nice out here, protected from
the city (secluded from the
elements) by the ruling redwoods.

i think i'll lumber
               around
                            the lumber and timber.

Five Haiku

1
time's certain curse
　fades in relativity's
future cessation

2
truth absolute
　flips over a coin to for
see the other side

3
salvation from
　society's secular
slavery: solitude

4
the earth's beauty
　eludes those who wallow in
the mire of greed

5
be passersby by
　bypassing the freeway to
financial freedom

Missing the Beat

the free way ends
and i pay the six dollar toll
cross the Golden Gate
but arrive in San Francisco
a few generations too late

Renaissance drums no longer *Beat*
Janis Joplin's counter-culture
cry of freedom no longer reverberates
throughout *The Haight's*
gentrified neighborhood
head shops record stores bars pubs
try to recapture the Summer of Love

Renaissance drums no longer beat
Harvey Milk's counter-culture
plea of equality no longer burrows
throughout *The Castro's*
gentrified neighborhood
token rainbow flags proudly fly
over drunken drag queens
leading street parades on their knees

William Carlos Williams provided—
        no letter of introduction
        no lsdpcpghbmdma to expand my consciousness
        no place to stay in the City by the Bay

    where (like Ginsberg)
  i too
have seen
my peers
"starving hysterical naked"
chasing the (white) dragon before
fixing themselves to

the temporary tempo of
a slowed drum circle
(a retarded circadian rhythm)

      where (like Ginsberg)
  i too
have seen
suburban junkies
"destroyed by madness"
languishing couch-ridden in
pharmaceutical comas before
dying slowly in
depressing drug den living rooms of
low-end
providers! dealers! servers! of life's hope

      where (like Ginsberg)
  i too
have seen
"visions! omens! hallucinations! miracles! ecstasies!"
or
more likely
certainties. axioms. palpabilities. mediocrities. miseries.

      and

      where (like Ginsberg)
  i too
am with you

  i too
am with you
in North Beach
crying chaos with Ferlinghetti

  i too
am with you
in the Tenderloin
trying madly not to succumb

   i too
am with you
in Mid-Market
being swept off the street

   i too
am with you
in the Mission
demurring the oppressive Ellis Act

   i too
am with you
in the Mission
serving coffee not the cops

   i too
am with you
in the Mission
dodging the Google mastodons

   i too
am with you
on the Embarcadero
expiring in gridlock aborting time

   i too
am with you
at the Ferry Building's clock tower
snapping photos capturing time

   i too
am with you
at Rincon Park
eating lunch from a brown paper bag

   i too
am with you
in the shadow of Cupid's Span
standing as a martyr

(to the place where
Tony Bennett left his heart)

   i too
am with you
on the Bay Bridge
stretching across the sea for eternity

   i too
am with you
on *The 80, 580*, and *5*
California ground

   i too
am with you
as i amicably depart San Francisco
Nevada bound

but i think i'll
take my punctured
bleeding heart
with me

it
may come in handy
somewhere
down the road

my still beating heart
may come in handy
down the road

Big Little Reno

damp cigarettes
mask
day old puke
rotting through indolently raked shag rugs

the BIGGEST LITTLE city
in the world
smells of the seventies

shick sideburns and yellow tinted shades
filter light
       p e e king
       through
              tiny seams
              in silver curtains
                      decaying
                      under
                      neon graves—
                      deserted
                      (like a dazed divorcée
                      in search of
                      the Comstock Lode)

Yosemite

someone tell the mountains
that Summer is on the way,
charging sidesaddle
atop a white mare
let loose from Spring's stable.

someone tell the mountains
that Summer is on the way,
racing thru the valley
with empty saddlebags
chock-full of unmet ransom demands.

someone tell the mountains
that they suffer from Stockholm Syndrome,
a hostage-friend to Winter's powerful curse,
clinging to beauty like an aging starlet,
another pinup clutching last month's forgotten calendar page.

someone tell Winter
that it's June the Twenty-Eighth,
time to set the mountains free,
let the snow melt away
and return unto the sea.

My Turn (Abridged)

unaccompanied by
darkness, i, a-part with the road,

share only pensive thoughts of
freedom with myself and the

cosmos. lessons of Jean-Paul
Sartre traipse the dun fantastic: a

reminder that we—alone on this
rock—are condemned to be free

with no other destinies than the
ones we forge ourselves. nearing

the microcosm of American
gluttony, Hoover Dam weeps;

neon perennials bloom, arising
from valley heights. a solitary tear

escapes my wearied eye, softly
rolling down my unshaven cheek.

the Strip leaves me speechless,
searching for suitable words

(asking myself),
"is it my turn now?"

(answering myself)
now, it's my turn.

ROUTE TWO
LAS VEGAS AWAKE

Paradise (Next

my accession
(into Paradise)

ushers not
the same raucous enthusiasm

greeting an impending bachelor party
carrying bundles of bills to Larry Flint's Hustler's Club.

my accession
(into Paradise)

ushers not
the same guileless eagerness

greeting a retired baby boomer couple
carrying comp tickets to *Cirque du Soleil: The Beatles Love*.

my accession
into *paradise* (next exit Summerlin)

unpretentiously ushers
heedless Red Rock Canyon resigning its rule over the dark night,

altruistically abdicating to the colossal unincorporated lights
searing the barren valley of hubbub.

Las Vegas Awake

the balding suit throws money
at the fake-boobed Ukrainian

bartendress as the hopeful
gamer inserts cash into the

slot. no winners here. on
television, Laird Hamilton

paddle surfs past the sound of
the Great Oz proclaiming his

magnificence. crashing waves
prevail. Stella quenches my

thirst as an imaginary
longboard carries my mind

from destinations known
back to worlds of fantasy

envisioned only in locked-door
dreams. a scream. uninvited

alarm's inconvenient reminder
spoils sanity. crashing sound

waves return reality, sending
subtle signals to hourglass

sands. time. slipping. sliding.
falling. gravity prevails. a lift?

with tips, the laws of physics
defied. the balding suit left

stiff. cock but no tail.
foreboding clouds abduct the

day's last moments. Westwind
yields not as Thor descends

unrestrained on the valley.
rain. departed zephyr spawns

an eerie, harmonious calm.
city slumbers. silence survives.

darkness reigns, savoring each
second until sunlight usurps.

first rays creek in window cracks,
signaling insomnia's sway over

Sin City's sleepless shadows.
Sin City's sleepless shadows.

tick tock.
tick tock.

restless desert residents desert rest.
awake.

Dream to Sleep

every
    (w)here
      here
        (t)here   vegas *frightens*

s t r u n   g   o   u   t clones[clones]
sur—flatbilled—round
new era (dog tags)
t i t d u n d
 w s e   t r e
slightly ri
       g
       h
       t d
         a
          n
           g
           l   a l i
            e   e   n
            starbucks d g
            safe caffeine
            (atthesamerateas)
            amphetamine.

the doctor says the doctor says the doctor doctor says says:
"are you are you clean? how 'bout some benzodiazepine?"

xanax **screams**
to
adderall junkies |=++++++++++++++=> fixated
                          on gaming machines
dream   [perhaps]
to
sleep.

Valleys of Fire

unrestrained independence awakes
my conscious mind exudes instant
ecstasies understood only by my
subconscious. swiftly fleeing the

security of my bedsheets, outside
cloudless sky leaves unrestrained sun
sending boiling beams of ultraviolet
radiance to the torrid terra firma,

superheating the cement wasteland
of desert sprawl. khaki stucco houses
parody pueblos, stacked atop each
other like Lego lands constructed by

the creative minds of school children.
escaping east, i lack objective and
soon find myself alone in the
wilderness adjoining Lake Mead,

drawn to the solace of nature. the
unmarked single-lane road stretches
into the expanse, meandering
between mountains and slithering

sideways like the serpent tempting
Jesus in the desert. without notice, the
paved path ends, presenting me with
only a barren, gravel road. do i follow

the path of pebbles and seek
destinations unknown or take the
return road to the splendors of
Sin City and set my soul alight?

the choice seems obvious.

rejecting the temptations of the world,
i proceed down the road less traveled
thru *valleys of fire* and reconnect with
abandoned Anasazi spirits before the

Arrowhead Trial hands me, scorching,
over to I-15 South and back into Las
Vegas. with no reason to sigh, I can
only reply, *"Robert Frost was right."*

and *that* has made no difference at all.

Beating Las Vegas

Las Vegas
you are
the slumlord of sanity
the pimp of perfidy
leasing your chimerical euphoria
by the hour

Las Vegas
you are
the playground of fantasy
the defalcator of chastity
molesting gullible rubbernecks
stripped naked by your lustrous beguilements

Las Vegas
you are
the marker of guise
the dealer of demise
occupying lines of oxidized steel
abandoned in haste by your re-virgined harbingers

Las Vegas
you are
the epitome of excess
the parlayer of success
sharing erstwhile stories of shame with no one
but your sanguine self

Las Vegas
you are
the American dream
the temple of agleam
glowing irradiant on the face of your unsent postcards
flaming aphotic on your wearied, deceitful heart

beating, beating, defeating ...

Starving

defeated under cover of
an unwashed patchwork quilt,
a handmade household heirloom

willed with teeming intentions,
a mother of two catnaps,
cemented atop a cowhide couch.

her ostracized offspring nettle, demanding dinner.

momentarily awaking
in yellow haze from a benzo stupor,
the mother musters enough energy

to update her Facebook status
before skyrocketing back
into holistic hibernation.

her spurned sucklings abide, starving (for something).

The Feast

```
        HUNGRY
        U
HUMANS  N
        G
        R
        Y
            T
            H
FOCUSED     D
   N        M
            S
            E
            L
            V         O
        DESCEND
            S
RED             Q
O               U
CASINO  BUFFET
K               U
            LIKE
                S
        D
VULTURES
        M
        A
        N
        DAILY
        I
CARRION
        G

[LUNCH]
```

Leftovers

desperation cloaks hope's silent cry—

a frail woman wearing years beyond her age
(and an *I Love Las Vegas* baseball cap)
sifts silently through trash bin scraps ...

moments later, she joyfully emerges
with a half-full can of beer
(abandoned by an inebriated tourist)
and without hesitation chugs it.

desperation cloaks hope's silent cry—

a frail woman wearing years beyond her age
(and an *I Love Las Vegas* novelty tee)
sits motionless in a scooter of mobility
embracing a square placard: *Disabled Veteran Needs Help* ...

moments later, she graciously accepts
a half-eaten bean burrito
(gifted by a well-intentioned tourist)
and without hesitation grubs it.

desperation cloaks hope's silent cry—

Fremont Street's victims feed on leftovers:
strangers' discarded American Dreams.

situation: bleak.

The Discarded Queen

snugged safely
in Summerlin's security

streetlights quiver
(off and on)

a half-moon away
day abdicates

to night
on The Strip

an old queen
pushes

through calm
Tropicana water

awaiting arrival
of today's trendy trade:

twenty-ones
(engaging in

egregious gossip)
espy only themselves

steaming
the discarded queen

(wrinkled and worn)
dealt no more

Bad Music

bass sounds box in stereotypes
sharing smoky secrets.

synthetic cymbals click,
invading elusive cliques.

escape?
no. it's the place.

beer bust bracelets bring bottomless beverages,
save top-shelf spirits.

born this way, a genderfuck lip-syncs stale pop,
selling drag show shots for dollar tips.

[fuck you fake Lady Gaga.
i liked you better when you were Madonna.]

a sole hipster shows himself,
rescinds a single.

tip sent & intended
for a stiff Scotch.

bartender repents;
dead president kept.

straight into slots,
games control

like brokeback
down lows

cloistering
life away.

Oh No (The Second Coming)

Las Vegas bachelor parties birth a testosterone fueled mob mentality: mass hysteria driven by one d-bag's quest for snatch and ridden by the rest. Drunken drunkies [fifteen in number]

descend straight on Stratosphere's Cirque du Soleil-like show, vampire style, sucking a Bite. Sapphire's strippers in sight. Bellicose blue-balled-stags rambunctiously board the White

Whale carrying a license for lewdness that surfaces inside seedy strip shows, seducing shitfaced suckers. Destination: The Luxor. New York & L.A. *partiers* represent Jersey. Soundtrack:

Springsteen. Born in the USA blasts. Blown speakers crack. Bachelors all tonight. Rings hidden. Bands of commitment gone. Idol wannabes' song. Cinderella's limos at midnight arrive to

drive those still alive to *glory days* [now night] filled with bimbos whose poles arouse trolls. For our reality show contestants still rolling on molly, four hours of *exotic* dancing doesn't satisfy.

It's on to Déjà vu Showgirls, where live titties are the second coming ... coming ... cumming ... oh ... oh ... oh ... ooooooooooh! Save it for a cold shower tomorrow when sober sanity squeals,

"Hell no."

Heart of the Coconut: The Faux Colossus

malapropos palms mirthfully surround Lady Liberty's Las Vegas doppelgänger as she distends from the depths of a foot-deep mote

and stands erect as the centerpiece of a comic book Manhattan skyline. wind sweeps psalms of sadness across the façade of

impostor Ellis Island, deflecting the pain of the *"tired and poor"* and rejecting the pleas of a *"homeless, tempest-tossed"* woman who grips

with both hands a neatly written cardboard sign that unabashedly broadcasts: PLEASE HELP. I JUST WANT TO GET HOME TO MY DAUGHTER.

strip scenes rustle herds of *"huddled masses"* from destination to destination under the guise of American Dreams, while beneath

replica representations of Eiffel Tower, Brooklyn Bridge, and Roman Colosseum a labyrinth of dank flood tunnels wreaks *"wretched*

refuge" for hundreds of displaced indigents whose American Reality reeks stagnant water and putrid body waste. but at *"sunset gates"*

abides my dream: transcending American indifference by standing as an open *"golden door,"* glowing as a beacon of freedom, where,

in harmony, you and i *"breathe free,"* sharing the world, united in communal exile. in my dream, we share the world in exile as one.

HOT SEXY GIRLS

the heat takes hold
and melts you from
the inside out (like
little plastic army
men succumbing
to the incandescence
of your sister's easy
bake oven and
metamorphosing into
nothing more than
green globs of
hardened, toxic goo).

forgotten pop-culture
icons from a wholesome
era resurface in an
ill-fated attempt to
reclaim past glories.

like Canadian geese
flying to warmer
climates, flocks of tourists
assemble in intimate
showrooms and fork
over big bucks to
recapture perished past.

neon-colored street walkers
slap stripper cards
against the deck
        shove them in your face
        try their best
        to entice you
        to buy
        HOT SEXY GIRLS.

multi-colored drunken hookers
slap hands
against each other's asses
        shove them in your face
        try their best
        to entice you
        to buy
        "hot sexy girls"
        a drink.

faux alcoves
of Rome
and Venice
manifest
a travesty
of authenticity
resurrecting
man-made illusions
of thousands
of years
of culture
via counterfeit canals
fraudulent fountains
reflect
LED signs
LCD screens
selling all
you can eat
buffets late
nite live
shows.

outside the Flamingo
microcosms of madness
        mimic reality
        increase instant insanity
        multiply mass hysteria.

following advice
Raoul Duke and i
forget folly
ride the crest
of a massive wave
lurching over
las vegas
boulevard

until—
    it bre
        a
           k
              s

leaving us flying
over dancing clouds
(reeling and swooping)
    knowing
    the entire time
    we had pushed
    our luck
    a bit too far.

i know now that we pushed our luck too far.

Govern or? (The Con of Sin)

Immobile again.
Lacking inspiration.
Deliberation
without motivation.
Absent.
Transient.
Tiny motion?
A prosaic location?
Can fix this fragment.

In Madison
the Nightwatchman descends
raging against the machine.
Worlds away
the Optimator
taps out.
Wonder Twins
try to entice
incite wagers.

Sanguine stakes
pledging parlays
for a lay.
An ante of assets
for some ass.
Senses stimulated
on a long shot.
Fickled fate
in a money shot.

Bet Makers
miss the Mark
treading heavily
on rocks of ice.
Melting.

Evaporating
like pensions.
Funds dissolving.
Derivatives decapitating.

Headless unions
rally.
Sway.
Say.
ParLay.

2day
workers reunite.
Incite what's right.
Write hisherstory
lines of unison
undone by governors.

Govern or?
We! Us! U$!
E-gypped.

Wes(t) falls for the
con of
sin
when
Lib-E-A.

Again.
I sit.
Immobile.

Absent.

Noodled

misplaced palm trees sanguinely map
boulevards from City Center to seaside sand.
the trail delivers me beach's end, where

revealed in Red Rock Canyon's glands only
oceanless desert sand. unwilling to succumb
to disappointment's oblong cry, i hastily grab

my zipperless—and favorite stick—and blindly
charge a swelling dune as if it were the last
wave. but its stoic disregard for my mere

presence graciously repays by launching me
orbitsville. my flimsy fuselage eats it at the
foot of Keystone Thrust, leaving me noodled.

A Lonely Haiku

buried in desert
sand, a seashell missing the
sea waits to be heard

Lost City

Converging deserts merge, unite, and grab each other by the hands as Set takes roll: Mojave! Sonoran! Great Basin!

Leaving behind Grand Canyon, Red River sweeps the desert and descends on Black Canyon, bringing life! pioneers! farms! to neighboring valleys and basins.

Mesa House Anasazi natives dwell in pueblos manufacture baskets mine salt trade food goods for Four Corners mountain pottery coastal turquoise.

                                                           (Life is good.)

Drought arrives.
Crops fail.
Malnutrition reigns.
Abandonment triumphs.

                                                        The city is lost.

Time passes. Enter the Mormons.

Religious pilgrims dwell in homes raise cotton operate stores provide food lodging for trailblazers following the Old Arrowhead.

St. Thomas* thrives at the junctions of the Muddy and Virgin Rivers where settlers peacefully cohabit with the Southern Paiutes and effectively end the Indian slave trade.

                                                         (Life is good.)

Time passes. Enter the Bureau.

Merging deserts converge, unite, and grab hands as Hugh
  Lord takes roll: Mojave, Sonoran, and Great Basin present
  and accounted for.

Saying goodbye to Grand Canyon, Colorado River sweeps the
  desert and descends on Black Canyon only to find Hoover
  Dam blocking its path.

Water arrives.
Crops fail.
Progress reigns.
Abandonment triumphs.

The city is lost.

The city is lost to those who wait for the river to run dry before
  crossing, needlessly missing meditative reflections

tendered by the changing bank
rendered by the changing bank.

---

*As a result of the drought experienced by much of the American West during 11 of the last 14 years, Lake Mead water levels have reached historic lows, and the 60 feet of water that once covered St. Thomas has subsided, revealing foundations, cisterns, and tamarisk. Studies show that the megadrought of the 12th and 13th centuries—which struck the same region and led to the decline of the Ancestral Puebloans, or Anasazi—was not as severe as the one expected in the near future.

Neon Roses

stone suburban parapets proficiently protect
  imprisoned municipal migrants beneath
    snow littered

mountain peaks of desert heat in sterile stucco shelters
  whose only variant the color of trim surrounding
    second floor

windows of time quickly commuting fifteen
  miles or forty-five minutes eastbound down
    charleston metamorphosing

martin luther king appropriating i-15 to paradise: the
  fabulous las vegas strip shows and gaming floors—
    cha ching—

of faux metropolises magically mimicking cultured cities
  stemming with taciturn tourists touting the authentic
    replica arc

de triumphant eiffel tower of babbling bellagio
  fountains flowing freely from lake mead to new york
    harbor's lady

liberty through venetian canals and valleys of king tut's tomb
  deeply dug deficits dooming dealers of draw poker to a
    luxorious life

of fleecing frustrated family men and women
  dancing dangerously close to naked extinction
    surviving solely

on the static sounds of a hapless hope fed by the
  unquenchable appetites of stingy slot machines and
    russian roulette

wheels spinning chambered webs of a vanquished
   doom blooming fully beneath a bounty of
     neon roses

revealing unconquerable odds hungrily harvested
   by rows of craps tables irrigated with plastic
     cow chips

whose intrinsic value seemingly reflects vibrantly
   useless monopoly money flippantly flung like a pair of
     dice drenched

with the last drop of blood forfeited by
   the fatted calf of greedy gamblers to
     callous casinos

Chasing Ghosts

escalator ascends
from gaming floor
to hotel entrance

metal rolling fire door
blocks access
to 1850

trespassing—
that's just
a misdemeanor

breaking & entering—
that's
a felony

but Gonzo said:
*"go straight
for the jugular"*

blocks away
on courthouse steps
i can hear my lawyer say:

*"as your attorney
i advise you to take the ~~mescaline~~
stairs back down and exit"*

there's
gotta be
another way

or am i just roaming
these ~~Mint~~ Binion escalators
chasing a ghost?

a suicidal ghost with
gun in mouth
phone in hand

~~inspiring~~
expiring
a generation

there's
gotta be
another way

NO
OTHER
WAY—

it's time to let ghosts go
it's time to let sleeping ghosts lie
it's time to quit chasing ghosts

Burning Ocean

A cool front circulates the desert, sending swirling cyclones through the streets of suburban Summerlin.

Opposition Jupiter Optimus Maximus dominates the nighttime sky, passing judgment on the earthly realm and swiftly sending jovial justice to those seeking verisimilitude.

Enter Cassiopeia—circling, circling, circling—swimming through the celestial sphere on her throne of torture, upside down half her life: a suspended symbol of her own vanity, vanishing by dawn's early light.

Daylight defeats darkness as Ra rises over the valley, revealing Red Rock Canyon and painting a deep, midnight-blue empyrean sky in my western backyard.

I have not slept in what seems like weeks and fear that I am losing touch with reality.

In this town, distinguishing between fantasy and reality is already difficult enough.

My mind will not stop.
  Thoughts arise like solar flares escaping the surface of the sun.

What am I doing in the desert?

Did I really leave life behind?
  Or had life left me behind long ago?

And where the fuck did I park *The Lincoln*?

The day is new and the future unwritten; but the places I have been, etched on the Internet for electronic eternity, already seem like a forgotten memory from another lifetime.

Time rears its relative head, and I jump a beam of light,
  transporting myself through a quantum tunnel back to the past.

260 million years ago, on the same spot I just departed, I am on
  an island, sitting on the beach, watching the birth of the Late
  Permian sun over the cold, thawing ocean.

The world is changing.
  Boulder is burning.

California is combusting.
  Elvis' soul is on fire.

Viva Las Vegas!
  Viva, Las Vegas.

Somewhere

tick tock.
tick tock.

seconds steal time,
hawking them at

the universal pawn
shop of special

relativity where
heaven is a *"fairy*

story" for those
afraid of the dark.

my beam of light
drops me off—

somewhere ...

Melody #87

wild-eyed hipsters awake rapidly (cold and wet), roll out of bed
furiously, and start the day's quest (reacting), futilely navigating

through self-constructed mazes of exile, driven to backstreet
black market fixes and simultaneously descending upon locked-

door rooms of privacy, waiting patiently in the queue for the
next rides on soiled, solitary magic mattresses that float

incandescently off hardwood floors of hope, guided blindly by
anxious Aladdins who serve dreams within dreams and hearken

Delphi for elucidation while traveling backward in ecstasy,
tantric trips of transcendental proportions fabricate reality and

progenerate mystifying reflections ricocheting violently off
broken mirrors of perception, two fists of fury swoop down like

a tornado—stabbing, omitting, forgetting—and skate
spellbound to lands of imprisoned fantasy, glorious

manipulation without reprieve but owning no guilt like a little
girl blaming her brother after breaking his toy car, couch surfers

riding borrowed waves stolen from brothers left standing at the
shore, alone, destined to watch grains of microscopic sand slip

through fingers like a Gibson disappearing into a black hole of
selfish desire where painful truths discover sidewalk's end, a

lonely place where cruelness supersedes kindness and
unknown adversaries arise, leaving behind martyrs that befall

disappeared daemons while spirits sit idly on parole, watching
drops of dignity float away on rainbowed balloons expanding

into the clouds, converging with Icarus, and plummeting into
the sea with shattered memories and forgotten dreams that

echo broken melodies, crying out from depths of doubt and
resurrecting life with every wave that crashes into the shore.

forgotten memories recall shattered dreams,
reborn when each wave reaches the shore ...

He Ain't Heavy; He's My Brother

Insomnia, my new best friend, keeps me company as another novel day arrives into my timeless world. *The Lincoln*, feeling refreshed after overcoming a bout of flat tire, begs to be driven. We cruise down *The 515* with no destination in mind, and before I realize it, she has taken me downtown.

The newly restored neon signs of what is now called *The Fremont Street Experience* attempt to revivify *Glitter Gulch*, the western end of Fremont Street seen in nearly every movie or television show that wants to capture the lights of Las Vegas.

Now, a giant canopy covers the street, which is shut off to vehicular traffic, and pedestrians move from casino to casino under the safety of a covered, four-block-long open-air shopping mall, complete with bright lights and Viva Vision LED show.

While carelessly wandering past the Four Queens and attempting to ascertain what cosmic event of unparalleled importance drew me here, I spot an African-American man favoring a well-defined limp. He makes eye contact with me and slowly approaches.

I have two choices: (1) quickly flee across Casino Center Boulevard like an ignorant racist and ditch him in a crowd of people; or (2) wait like a caring, empathetic human being and engage him in conversation.

Allow me to present Marine Staff Sergeant Tony (he asked me to redact his last name). Nine years ago, Sgt. Tony lived a *normal* life with his girlfriend in Wichita, Kansas. Today, he refuses to contact her, afraid that he is going to "choke her out."

Inspired by the "heroism and patriotism" of the New York Fire Department on 11 September 2001, Sgt. Tony immediately enlisted in the Marines and was deployed to Iraq as part of the first wave of the 2003 invasion.

Sporting barely a day's worth of stubble on his face and a freshly shaved head, it is hard to tell that Sgt. Tony has been on the streets, sleeping in bathrooms and bathing in sinks, since his discharge from the hospital six days ago after going into insulin shock.

"I was just walking around, minding my own business, and my vision goes out," he says with a certain uneasiness in his voice.

"Then a SWAT team shows up and takes me down. I woke up in the hospital ... had no idea I'm diabetic."

The thirty-six year old vet's face is hardened and worn, displaying lines of life usually only apparent in someone twice his age, and his voice carries the angry wisdom of a man who has experienced too much pain for a single lifetime: "People roll dice, a thousand dollars a roll. Tip a girl with fake titties a hundred bucks, but they won't buy a vet a cup a coffee."

While on patrol in Afghanistan in 2008, an IED exploded near Sgt. Tony's Humvee, shrapnel struck his head, and he lost his left eye. An empty, collapsed socket is all that remains. "I came out here to Vegas to go to Nellis to get my eye fixed," he says with a newly discovered sense of confidence. "I'm not leaving 'til the mission's complete."

But Sgt. Tony's mission seems futile at this point. The maxillofacial surgeons at Nellis Air Force Base's 114-bed medical treatment facility, run in a joint venture with the Department of Veterans Affairs, refuse to operate until his diabetes are under control.

Fresh diabetes diagnosis (and homelessness) aside, Sgt. Tony's greatest challenge, however, seems to be overcoming mental illness. He says that when he returned home from his third tour in Afghanistan he spent four months in a psych ward and received no therapy or counseling. "They asked me if I heard voices. I said, 'Sometimes,'" he admits as he looks over his shoulder and then hides his face from a passing security guard.

"They told me I was bipolar and had Post-Traumatic Stress Disorder," he continues after a moment. "Hell, I'm schizophrenic."

Doctors prescribed him a cocktail of psychotropic drugs: Lithium, Zoloft, Seroquel, and Thorazine. Sgt. Tony no longer takes his meds and is depressed and suicidal.

He says his bronze star and two purple hearts mean nothing to him. "It's not about those symbols. I love this country and would do it all over again," Sgt. Tony expresses with pride. "But I hate the government and just want my eye back."

The sun slowly rises over the canopy of Fremont Street, and the neon lights flicker no more. Sgt. Tony hobbles off into the distance, a shadow of his previous self and a hidden casualty of the Iraq and

Afghan wars. A Musak version of the Beatles' "Penny Lane" plays over the loudspeakers.

   I sit, and meanwhile back.

   I sit, and meanwhile ...

Body Bags

the body bags keep coming home
   but the caskets remain concealed
middle-east streets the combat zone
   roadside bombs line the battlefield

the body bags keep coming home
   no exit strategy prepared
our country's future placed on loan
   the fertile crescent scorched and seared

the body bags keep coming home
   no immediate end in sight
the seeds of terror firmly sewn
   by freedom's military might

the body bags keep coming home
   no army spouse should ever hear
that dreaded knock, the leading tone
   confirming a sacrosanct fear

the body bags keep coming home
   crusading tycoons the reason
no martyr could ever atone
   old glory's murderous treason

the body bags keep coming home
   let us shed a tear for the lost
till our souls have evolved and grown
   beyond warfare's damnable cost

Dizzy Math (The Thizz of Nature)

My beam of light returns me to the desert, an oasis:
  Calico Basin's saltgrass meadow, thriving in homeostasis.

Natural springs emerge from the base of sandstone cliffs,
  petrified sand dunes decorated with native petroglyphs.

Southern Paiutes displaced by the Homestead Act of '62;
  39,000 square miles stolen without further review.

Aboriginal homelands redistributed to settlers;
  a barren reservation, the gift to tribal elders.

Then, in 1938, the Small Tract Act passed;
  free fertile land for all, the Dust Bowl was aghast.

But now, the BLM wants the real estate back,
  paying 700 grand per acre or 3.5 million for each tract.

That's a hell of a lot more than they paid our Piaute brethren;
  a 1965 court judgment awarded 2 bucks an acre for Calico Basin.

Now all these numbers are making me dizzy;
  it's time to forget myself and drop Tu-weap's ecstasy.

Rollin from acre to acre;
  rollin on the *thizz* of nature.

The ~~Myth~~ Meth of Change

sphinx sits atop
watchtower
spying friday night.

vegas in
lock down town up town
a riddle guarded sits watch.

jonesing tweakers' giant pupils
wander nervously through
sin city's bloodshot eye socket,

darting and pacing
the pavement
for change:

hope
don't
pay

[the rent]

spent on
the meth of
the masses.

a pocketful
of change
remains.

promised change
elusive as
promised lands:

gritting teeth in desert sands.

A New Day

at dawn
Casino Center
bus stop
brings out
a cast of
characters unseen
in one's daily stream:
a recovering
crack addict
whose wife
chooses rock
over life.

pipe replaced by can
(brown paper bag in hand)

Jamal says
he can
no longer watch
his lover
turn backroom tricks
for her next dirty fix.

transit on approach,
roach nearly toked

my new friend
bumps my fist
(bus token in hand)
and rides away,
gliding on
Vegas hope:

a new day.

Las Vegas Awake (Reprise)

chasing melodies unwritten
from Spring's mountains
to Fremont's experience,

the new day bestows
its inglorious promise:
a sacred pledge.

adventure marshals in
orange clad
case numbers.

bracelets contain
chain
restrain.

freedom revoked by
addiction's
choke hold.

a trap?
a choice?
a reminder.

daydreams resuscitate
ephemeral arias of retroinspection
but soon secede

to nightdreams
transposing fantasia's locks
into keys of rhapsody.

tick tock. tick tock.
restless desert residents desert rest.
awake.

Racing Nowhere

The checkered flag rapidly drops, signaling the start of today's race for survival.

Commuters travel east on Charleston, fleeing suburbs' safety for the *security* of Strip employment, where the balance of life hangs from a tiny thread dangling from the top of the Stratosphere.

The state of the economy—rising unemployment, debt, foreclosures, and evictions—stands as the biggest threat to the mental health of the valley community and contributes to the highest suicide rate in the nation, nearly twice as high as the rest of the country.

It is easy to see why euthanized apparitions stayed only three days and in order to survive needed a trunkload of drugs that *"looked like a mobile police narcotics lab."*

Once the Disney-like magic of the marketing wears off and the allure of the bright lights fades to day, the city kidnaps and her residents cling to the last remnants of life, abiding like a swatted fly whose broken left wing furiously flickers until it realizes the gift of flight is gone.

I long for life outside the manufactured realities of the Las Vegas Boulevard of Broken Dreams.

I long for the real streets of Rome, where in a bar beneath the remains of the Colosseum an Italian man plays guitar and sings in broken English *Light My Fire*—not a faux Coliseum where Cher executes stale pop to sell-out crowds paying five-hundred a head.

I long for the real cuisine of Venice, where family-owned restaurants serve home-cooked meals and house-wines from local vineries—not mass produced all-you-can-eat casino buffets sitting atop copied canals.

I long for the real perfume of Lower Manhattan and my daily stroll from Midtown skyscrapers to a Chelsea office overlooking the Hudson—not a roller coaster ride around a replica Metropolis skyline lifted from a post World War II Superman comic.

I long for the real flavor of the Pacific's salt-water on my tongue—not the essence emanating from the tears of salt-water sweat rolling down my fraying face: hemorrhaging perspiration courtesy the intense, ardent desert.

I long for the open air of the road and the freedom of not knowing where each day will take me.

My nomadic spirit cannot sit still.

The sirens sing songs of hope,
joyously luring my return to the road.

ROUTE THREE
HOLLYWOOD ALLURE

Pilot Season

i'm headed to Los Angeles
with a
television guest star
who has a SAG card and
too few IMDb credits
two to be exact
to his name

i've been told that
it's pilot season
where landing a recurring role
on a shitty sitcom is
an especially welcomed fate
for the
indie recording artist slash
television guest star

i'm not worried
that we have no place to stay

it's pilot season

and some of his Hollywood
guest star *"friends"*
have said we can
crash with them

i'm sure it will be fine but
i'm packing my tent and
i'm packing my sleeping bag (just in case) and
i'm packing my—

    mostly his stuff
    into *The Lincoln's* trunk

it's huge:

   the amount of his stuff
   (and *The Lincoln's* trunk)

gangster types obviously
selected the Town Car for
the sheer amount of dead and/or live
—i've pegged it at eleven—
bodies that could be
stashed easily in there
or
clothes-cases
shoe-cases
guitar-cases
vinyl-record-cases
desktop-computer-cases
and
just-cases
full of every kind of
fashion accessory known
to (and for) the
heterosexual hipster effete emo indie recording artist slash
television guest star
with a SAG card and
too few IMDb credits
two to be exact
to his name

i'm still not sure where to stow
my dirty underwear

but i'm not worried
it's pilot season

Soon Wilshire Soon

carefree road runners soar
down *The 5* in search of Angels
until Wile E. Coyote intervenes

with an Acme explosive,
transforming the tactile tract of
tar into a paved parkwaying lot

overrun by sedentary snails.
(California traffic travels at two
 tempos: 186,000 miles per

second or absolute atrophy.)
speed limit signs vanish into the
void, scratched from roadsides

and terminated like the T-1000
by the Gubernator('s budget
cuts). commuters clog the San

Diego Freeway, firing fossil fuels
and wasting treasures of time in
traffic. held captive against my

will—a slave to the city's daily
demands—my patience grows
thin as saltwater dreams

detonate my dome, sending
signals of secession to the sacra
at the base of my spine.

waiting
for Wilshire Boulevard,
waiting.

sneaking
forward, slowly
sneaking.

closing
on my target, casually
closing

(like a battalion
of foot soldiers creeping across
Settentrione).

retreating,
not today:
proceeding.

Wilshire will soon
supervise my passage
to the sea.

soon, Wilshire will
shepherd
the sea unto me.

Past Palisades Park

Palisades Park pushes me over stony scarps
onto a pedestrian passageway that spans the PCH,
sending me the sands of Santa Monica Beach.

Subterranean sapphire saliva disguises
cloudless azure skies; snow-white
caps collide with strand's shallow shore.

Schools of social sharks stride up and down
and down and up the seaboard, savoring
a summer stroll of superfluous satisfaction.

Sunbathers sit subservient to Sun's smile,
slowly scorching their spotted sheaths,
unscathed by the seething scarlet stains.

Surfers assemble side-by-side; soon, the
looming swell will surface and scores
of stoked Slaters will step into liquid.

Suddenly, a sundry of seraphim schlepps me
to Svarga, sentencing me to a stretch of satiety
superior to any subsequent metempsychosis.

So, I surf out past the breakers,
leave the past behind.

Out past the breakers,
the past passes away.

Los Angeles Outlook

today's Times unexpectedly
shot the forecast
into my eye:

70 & sunny ...
with an
80% chance of s   m   o   g

left with no other choice
to the Hollywood Hills
i went for a hike

and upon reaching
cloud's rest promptly
rolled & lit a cigarette

       then pondered why it's
       illegal to smoke
       tobacco
inside]
       but
       legal to burn
       fossil fuels
              ]outside

    when again Downtown Los Angeles sighed

before gasping and exhaling
some more carbon die-ox-ide*
into the atmosphere

Carbon dioxide is the primary gas emitted through the combustion of fossil fuels. Since the start of the Industrial Revolution around 1750, human activities have added carbon dioxide and other heat-trapping gases to the atmosphere, which in turn have contributed substantially to climate change and caused Earth's surface temperature to rise.

Wannabes

1
Each afternoon,
hipster filmmakers
depart their parents' homes

(like grease moths
exiting the cocoon in
search of light or sugar),

ritualistically assemble
in Sherman Oaks coffee
houses with overpriced
Macbook Pros in tow, and
pretend to write the next
box office hit, gathering
not for their own benefit
but to the detriment of others:

for only we can see
the prominence of
their shared delusion.

Hiding behind his
Warby Parker Feltons,
which do not Jack
Kerouac a man make,
one myopic with no
imagination—they all
have little or no vision
or (in)sight—declares:

"*Ya gotta have a lot of money
if ya wanna do anything too crazy.*"

Then I laughed.

2
Each night,
I ritualistically park *The
Lincoln* on a residential
street in West Hollywood and
securely lock the doors and
wait for the auto headlights
to dim before turning away.

But tonight, at 2:07 a.m., snugged
comfortably in my overpriced bed at
Chateau Marmont, I awoke from that
nightmare, untangled my left arm
from the steering wheel and my
right foot from the brake pedal,
reclined myself a bit more, and
declared over and over again to
the half-awake television guest star
occupying the seat next to mine:

*"You can't do anything too
crazy without a lot of money."*

Then I laughed ...

grateful of my prescription
—an overabundance of imagination
and determination compounded with
intolerable eyesight of foresight
or inoperable 20/20 vision—
and tried to fall back asleep
in *The Lincoln's* cozy front seat,
counting not sheep but the seven
hundred twenty-two deeply
deceased Washingtons
(and one IMDb credit)
that I currently have to my name.

Hollywood Allure

        t
        h
        i
        s
        m
        o
        r
       ni
       ng
    i awoke and the zipper
<on my sleeping bag was broke>
<(n) dog hair and pot seeds>
<carelessly cultivated on the floor>
<of the apartment of the two>
<stoners who provided shelter last>
<night i was covered by the>
<morning light blasting through>
<the sliding glass balcony door i>
<spotted a stack of 45s sitting idly>
<atop a spindle stabbing the sky>
<with tone poems of color that>
<resonate from the subterranean>
<chamber of the concrete bunker>
<in the house that Nat built>

and
thus the allure of my Hollywood
                            reality

A Hollywood Rhyme

at rush hour, SAG seeking
shirtless studs insolently
step all over Satchmo
wishing upon a star (not

his) and weave through
crowds of star seeking
sightseers hoping to be
discovered: a morning jog.

despite condemnation
from television guest stars
(*"keep moving"*), i stop and
gaze at the supernova

encompassing Grauman's
Chinese and ingest the
pungent ersatz of fried
soylent green papayas

or tomatoes or hornets or
lanterns on the boulevard
everything's gone green: a
pending premiere. this

recipe does not bemuse as
the cacophonous touch of
fame to my sole reiterates
why i came: not for fame

but to remind that fate is
unkind when your dreams
only exist within the confines
of a classic Disney rhyme.

Meanwhile 1-($%#@&)

Meanwhile, in beautiful downtown Burbank ...

A major multimedia megacorporation
    —managed
    by a mickey mouse
    mostly possessed
    by the fruity man*
    promising
    the latest i-($%#@&) airminiplusproretina device—
bombards America's adolescents
with pre-fabricated pop ~~star~~starts
that grow up to be
tina smoking nude posing
drunk driving *yeyo* snorting
head shaving rehab living
bulimic petty addictive
thieves.

With other directors
in unison he screams:

"Capture the children.
Homogenize their heads.
Concoct a culture of consumers."

With sane defectors
in dissension I scream:

"Dreams do not come true at theme parks."

---

*On 24 January 2006, The Walt Disney Company agreed to acquire Pixar from majority owner Steve Jobs for $7.4 billion in Disney shares, making Jobs the largest individual shareholder of Disney. The deal also gave Jobs a seat on the Disney Board. Interestingly, Jobs had purchased Pixar from George Lucas on 3 February 1986 for $5 million. Jobs died on 5 October 2011 at the age of 56, leaving behind an estimated fortune of over $8 billion. Shortly before his death, the NY Times reported that "there is no public record of Mr. Jobs giving money to charity."

Stars in the Background

Each week,
hundreds of anonymous migrants
exit the bus agog
and fill the great hall in Burbank,
chasing stardom's call.

Their virgin faces mugshot
and provident forms measured
for a mere twenty-five,*
but no one here's rejected
regardless of shape, age, color, creed, or size.

Once the forms are filed
registration heralds
the paltriness of their rapidly razed given names
(no matter if it's Pitt, Longoria, or ~~Wayne~~ Morrison):
the *actors'* reward invisibility
with wretched hours
and minimum wages of the same.

But when the inexorable chasing ends
and stardom finally rings
with a role cast in stone
and typed neatly on a call sheet
under the simulacrum
of atmosphere and standins,
the ticket has been dispensed
on this cursory track to imminent fame.

And when the camera rolls
(and action declared),
each walking stereotype
(or cinematic wallflower),
with faith unseen
by any priest monk or nun,

proudly chants
(with unparalleled conviction)
the extra's mantra
beckoning infamy's reign:

it's better to be seen
briefly crossing the background
in a motion picture scene
than it is not to be seen
as a minute flashing blip
on the gawking talent scout's
ever changing radar screen.

*In May 2011, the Los Angeles City Attorney's Office, citing the 2009 Krekorian Talent Scam Prevention Act, informed Central Casting that the company risked prosecution unless it stopped charging photo-registration fees. While denying that it was subject to this law, Central Casting immediately stopped charging performers seeking background work.

Beverly Center: Empty—

the middle of the day
in they go
emptyhanded

hours later
out they come
emptyhearted

hushed voices
narrate the tale
shrieking wordless

logoed paper bags
the only witness
lewdly advertise

taste and waste
remunerated by
parking slips' validation

sought but unreturned
ardor prostrates
crumbled and forsaken

on the garage floor

A Narcissist on Santa Monica Beach

Treat with great skepticism
the TV guest star who

(while sitting on the beach)
misses the beauty

of an ocean sunset
in that he was too busy

preening in a mirror.

Echo cried;
Narcissus died;

and I'm standing
fearful of

those who gaze
but can't see

IT.

THEY

the sauna at The Y
where even

the Village People
dreaded to tread

beguiles
real estate brokers

prepping for a hard day
of swapping plots

for the haughty
naked eyeballs penetrate

bare backed Clydesdales
galloping erect

muscles pumped
winning L.A.'s clash

with self-image
a-part in the shower

i eschew
TheY

Meet Me

prowling
the grove
in hunt of
a 200 dollar
pair of jeans
an unknown
television guest star
delicately sips
a stiff caramel macchiato
from Starbucks
with the symmetry
of a ballerina

at home
in his natural habitat.
swigging
a two dollar black coffee
from Bob's
a fledgling
screen writer
cavorts
upon a flimsy
metal and wood chair
absorbing
the stage

in the penumbra
of the clock tower.
a presage solicits
passersby to
meet me
at Third and Fairfax

my apple fritter
nearly consumed.

Dirty Dirty Echo Park

the ancient bard
staggers sunset

from pub to pub
his dirty prose
echoes about the park

past the groucho Marxist
disposed on the corner
left bleeding by the skirmish
enriching himself and
ameliorating for right

maladroit cops and
wing-ed pies
grace Edendale
when Hollywood seizes
reign o'er the silver screen
stealing bathing beauties
swimming in shorts

supplanted by features
talkies take hold
of box office receipts
giving the slip to
anarchist communes

trust-funded hipsters
strut sunset
from pub to pub

infecting the park
their clothes dirty

Somnolent Stars

tonite on Yucca and Wilcox
the stars fall brightly

in the hallway
a lambasted
drag queen slumbers

outside Ed Wood's door

window ledges
typecast
unengaged street walkers

in chinos

Willie the Pimp
angles the porch
leasing doxies

for a twenty spot

a rapacious trick
bludgeons to sleep
the Fernwood Flasher

in a meretricious cage

hostages of fame
sanitize the narrative
of Hollywood disgrace

at the transubstantiated Lido
a television guest star comatose in the closet

DB on the Third Street Promenade

     green—
garbage dumpsters; tourists on the corner of the third street promenade.

     manna—
from heaven; spoon fed by the hand of god.

     domicile—
subconscious visions; apparitions of an undiscovered country spawn surreal illusions dancing around the cemetery.

     carolyn—
a seizure; another DB; supplementary DB without opportunity.

forensic unit—
     uncomfortable tension; the loss of gravity surrounds eager expectations wallowing in misery.

     shaking—
a cigarette; yellow tape circling the alley; red lights flashing; flashing fortuitous allusions as perceptions of reality ignore intimate intentions ricocheting under the brevity.

     life—
capital; cuisine; apparel; asylum; a warm place to sleep.

     time—
existing; expired; immutable sleep.

     death—
malicious misconceptions of a befuddled mystery pander to pathetic rationalizations floating around insanity.

      reminiscence of atrocity—
formidable frustrations of a vanquished humanity transcend
ambiguous aggravations emancipating captivity.

      carolyn—
another exiled individual; another from the streets; one more DB;
one more conquered american pipe dream; DOA on the corner
of the third street promenade; just another DB.

      why god?

Bernie the Homeless Guy

at two a homeless man
patrols the quixotic boundary
between Beverly Hills and West Hollywood

with the audacity
of a border patrol agent
on the Mexican line

he'll tunnel you
under the Center
from San Vincente to La Cienga

for some company
and a pack of smokes
he announces me

to a coterie of *aspiring* writers
languishing outside the Coronet
pretentious fucks fleeing

LIVE
NUDE
GIRLS GIRLS GIRLS

bread squandered
on a phony rack
modest Bernie reeling

ALIVE
BARE
POCKETS POCKETS

tracks my scent to Norms
his breakfast lurks
on the counter

L.A. Breakfast with a Professor Emeritus

at nine, L.A.
time, *Times* in hand,
the retired professor
sits alone at
the kitchen table
taking breakfast.
i quietly join him.

turning the page,
the byline
storyline
timeline
provides fodder:
ruminative fare.
Rousseau was a Marxist.

with the slapdash
zeal of a child,
he hurriedly
bites into
a slice of
cherry pie.
i eagerly join him

A Scene at Griffith Park

FADE IN:

EXT. GRIFFITH PARK - DAY

A TELEVISION GUEST STAR effortlessly hikes a trail on Mount Hollywood. A WRITER and a FORMER GAME SHOW CONTESTANT, both attired in improper footwear, follow behind, unhurried. The Television Guest Star pays little attention to his languishing companions.

>TELEVISION GUEST STAR
>Fucking pansies!

At mountain's summit, the Television Guest Star abruptly removes his shirt, revealing a six-pack of abdominal muscles. He catwalks on the lawn in front of Griffith Observatory, unaware of his surroundings, hoping, however, that others are aware of him. Moments later, the Writer and the Former Game Show Contestant arrive at entertainment industry's zenith, energized.

>TELEVISION GUEST STAR (CONT'D)
>All right, bros. Let's head back down.

Hungry, the Television Guest Star and the Former Game Show Contestant promptly descend the trail back down the hill, deserting the curious Writer. Replete, the Writer sojourns, digesting the aesthetic of his morning production:

A great dome coruscates in the unseasonably warm Los Angeles sun. Downtown reclines shrouded in linens of silken smog in the concrete basin below. Hollywood's most iconic lettered landmark juts unembarrassed from the hillside of puny Mount Lee. Snow caps *telegraph* peaks frolicking from Ontario to Cucamonga.

The Writer muses on the lawn in front of the observatory, aware.

FADE TO BLACK.

Mirrored Sunset

Sunday in Santa Monica
north of the pier
the wind recalls howling dead

the hushed Santa Ana wind
resurrects departed Afghan sand

it cremates precipitated ash and dust
ordered by generals to surround
neurotically lined crosses flank
star spangled draped plastic coffins encase
specters of unknown comrades fallen

a mirror image of Arlington
sheds its sepulcher for the west

[impotent to prevent eradication
a gulf away unwitting soldiers
engage for Middle East sovereignty]

Sunday in Santa Monica
south of the pier
the wind dismisses howling dead

the rabid Santa Ana wind
embalms lingering Mojave sand

it occupies chiseled muscle beach
ordered by talent agents to battle
stable swinging ropes clutch
cold steel barrels strengthen
armies of unrelenting Hollywood hopefuls

a mirror image of Tinseltown
dips its silhouette in the sunset

Pilot Season (Reprise)

with the final trophy dispensed
and red carpet rolled up

for yet another year
Hollywood frames its consideration

from honoring its bright stars
from casting its fresh faces

to regaling full of hubris
in its impending summer season

no one steps out of line
in the shadow of Disney's castle

wannabe hipsters pretend to write
and an extra perfects his entrance

leaving casting couches on the floor
homeless souls do plot their exits

while an unknown TV guest star
approaches a thousand Facebook likes

the Hollywood allure dissolves to memory
in the mercy of the night

Contentious Clouds

the mild Santa Monica sun
(guaranteed to the masses)
again lures me seaside.
before advancing onward,
my civic responsibility
requires me once more
to rollick
under Sol's gaseous glory.

Neptune majestically molds
a mild serf
while Hyperion upholds
his covalent covenant
with California
chargés d'affaires,
granting yet another day
of idiosyncratic elegance

to the multitudes.
in a twist of fate
(patently part of
the pact to provide
unprecedented pulchritude),
Disney ironically
co-opts Hyperion's handle
to promote its imprint

of bestselling books
to bairn demographics.
crossroads aside,
spreading solicitude
suddenly swells
straight through
my substance,
surrounding me

like sub-atomic positrons
circling the nucleus
of a hydrogen isotope
seconds after
the cyclopean explosion
of a singularity.
through friction,
Helios carefully

commands his chariot
across the sky,
skillfully steering
setting sun
as it disappears
on the horizon
and descends
into the sea,

delivering darkness
until tomorrow's dawn
and the leading rays
of the new-fangled
reborn sun.
contentious clouds
no longer hover
into my heart

to deliver
a deluge
of precipitation
but arise from oblivion,
adding a magnanimous stain
to my sunset sky.
clouds arise from oblivion
and magnanimously stain

my sunset sky.

ROUTE FOUR
BACKSTREET MARGINALIA

PRNDL: Transmission

Reverse is a mostly overrated gear except when
backing out of a car Park
a destructive relationship or
a pile of shit

i don't trust those who travel backwards to
recapture a parallel past
relive a bygone present or
recreate a reminiscent future

              (repeat, regress)

back to the places they've already been
back to the places they've already been

moving forward in Drive and letting
what's behind me
what's passed by me or
what's passed me by
stay a rearview mirror reflection of
Neutral receding lines
in *The Lincoln's* back window is
all that i trust is
all that i need

but before losing the only forward gear
that propels me in Low past
who i was and toward
who i will become

i'm gonna need a new transmission
              (or rhetorical strategy)

Rhymes of Ancient Mariners

Spartan scouts assemble by the sea,
Singing a paean to Poseidon.

Alexander pauses by the shore,
Sights silhouettes of brazen-hoofed horses

With manes of gold
Galloping across the skyline.

Rhymes of ancient Mariners
Resolutely ring from the Pacific's depths

And evaporate into the celestial sphere,
Delicately dancing across the atmosphere.

Condensating! Sublimating! Precipitating!
Delivering drops of life

Back down into the nadirs below.
In another gulf of time ...

Alexander pauses by the shore,
Sights brazen, black blankets of muck

Leaving behind a plume of rogue, deepwater droplets
Stretching mile after mile,

Refusing to dissipate
Despite deadly dispersants.

American addicts assemble by the sea,
Singing a paean to BP.

Rhymes of ancient Mariners
Resolutely ring from the Gulf's depths

And transform into tears of distress,
Dangerously dancing across the atmosphere.

Condensating. Sublimating. Precipitating.
Delivering sorrows of abuse

Back down into the nadirs below.
In time ...

Alexander pauses by the shore once more,
Sights silhouettes of brazen, liquid waves

Crashing into Sunset Cliffs
(With power unsurpassed).

High tides! Low tides! Riptides! A jetty!
Swells that reach far and vast.

Spartans come and addicts go,
Turn their backs on spiritual serenity,

Yet unconditionally it gives,
Freely gives of all its energy:

A love that is there for the taking,
A precious gift for all to share,

Rhymes of ancient Mariners
Resolutely ring, sing cries from the deep,

"I am the ocean,
Reach out to me if you dare."

I *am* the ocean,
Reach out to *me* if you dare.

Ocean Beach

the fire of life's ember
extinguishes in the dancing sea,
hatching the blackness of night,
antecedently acquitted from all

acumen and blame. the tide of
tomorrow clings profoundly to
its predestined timetable,
dutifully waning west (from

whence it came) before
succumbing to the night's
deliberately waxing dark moon,
held at bay by the curvature of

spacetime. homer tucks in his
unwritten words for the night as
ocean muses seduce his dreams
with swelling songs heard in

search of undiscovered paladins.
the night (oh calm night) sits
lonely, rebuffing the spot light,
sleeping by shadowy breaths of

life that recklessly gallop atop
waves of verity fueled by dire
chills of melancholy fears
exhaled by the city's indigent

who lie in want of a savior.
daybreak waits restlessly,
caressing salt white dew drops
(lost to the feral parrot

mimicking the distant barn owl's
evaporating hoo hoo hoo) that
slowly vibrate and indiscriminately
crash into splintered storm

windows promising little
protection from the new day's
imminent preamble. in relative
chorus (but three meridians away),

pavlov's bell rings rings rings,
signaling ignorant elites to
trade ephemerally their poorly
stocked eternities for an avaricious

fate (to be) determined by the
bazaar's bewitching derivatives.
back at ocean beach, sunup
chaperons the alchemy hour; a

morning set, spreading like a
virus carrying a redeeming love,
infects microcosmic militias of
unvaccinated freedom seekers, who,

while carving radical, develop
immunity from the assimilative
agitprop disseminated by the
smogbreathers of the new gilded age.

Hounds of Hell

Reluctantly readying myself for the weariness of the way ahead, I already regret exchanging the ocean's brisk breath, the comforts of the coastal sun, and my bucolic beach-bum life(style) for the rigidly relentless desert heat and sweltering summer sky.

Scorching western sun chases me like the Hounds of Hell hawking heathens through the Wild Hunt in Wistman's Wood.

Pushing onward, I compete not only with calefaction but also U.S. Border Patrol checkpoints—Fourth Amendment-Free Zones—near the Mexican border on Interstate-8 as temperatures in the Sonoran peak at 110 and federal agents subject all travelers to warrantless searches, sniffing out *illegal* drugs (and aliens).

Reports of the detention of *patients*, the confiscation of *medicine*, and the prosecution of federal drug charges surface, despite President Obama's promise not to pursue cases against medical marijuana beneficiaries.

Predator drones protect borders but homeland security does not protect against *"unreasonable searches and seizures."*

Frightened by my quickly eroding civil liberties,
I flee the hounds of hell.

I fly.

Log Cabin Lament

The temperature smacks one-fifteen
In degrees of dry desert sheen.
  Air is thin but thick as well;
  I do believe this is hell.
Perhaps it's just the Benzedrine.

Giant saguaro flips me off,
With middle finger he doth scoff.
  His evil eyes follow me
  Through sands of iniquity,
Like Humbert Humbert. Nabokov!

Hold on. Listen. What do you hear?
That voice—its message—isn't clear.
  Some thing, some thing, the Lord's Prayer,
  Something to eat, drink, and wear
Bleeds F.M. Christ from speaker's ear.

Do not worry, Scottsdale is near.
Promises of two-for-one beer
  Ease silent thoughts of despair
  And guide me to Satan's lair,
Where Log Cabin spells hidebound queer.

Superstition Ain't the Way

Newspaper headlines warn of danger here:
Missing hiker found near Lost Dutchman trail.
"Thar's gold in them thar hills" foretells folktale,
So near Superstition explorers leer
In search of treasure; dreams of wealth appear.
Coronado heeds not Thunder God's rail
Against transgressing sacred grounds' safe swale;
Soon, decapitated, ugly heads rear.
Here, newspaper headlines warn of danger:
Three hikers hunting lost treasure feared dead.
Bygone ghosts of ancestors bleed blood red
And, dying, declare life's final mission:
"Belief in Superstition leads, stranger,
To the belief in more superstition."

DARK AGES

Every home in Arizona is the same color: desert sand. Rust colored rocks replace green grass and take root in minuscule yards, painting a desaturated suburban landscape reminiscent of a 1950s black & white sitcom sponsored by Phillip Morris.

Evangelical Republicans—Tea Party favorites—seek to replace the color and diversity of America with a parochial uniformity similarly found in Southwestern sprawl and the sanitized, *wholesome* fantasy of the Golden Age of Television.

  turn off your TV
  america
  awake

(from your slumbers of amnesia)

  bury Tea Party ideals
  in the cemetery
  of our checkered past

(let us return not to the Dark Ages)

The Truth (From a Hotel Room in Flagstaff)

The Setup—
Former President Jimmy Carter on Larry King Live:
"A lot of gullible folks in the United States actually believe what Fox puts forward as facts when most of it is just complete distortions ... There has been a deliberate effort—again, referring to Fox Broadcasting—to inject the race issue into it."

Fox *News* commentator Bill O'Reilly* replied:
"So it seems Mr. Carter is not telling the truth, and it is beneath a former president to accuse FNC of injecting race into the political process as Carter does. Carter can simply not back up what he says ..."

The Truth—
Fox *News* commentator Glenn Beck** professed:
"This president has exposed himself as a guy, over and over and over again, who has a deep-seated hatred for white people ... Obama has a problem. This guy is, I believe, a racist."

News Corp CEO Rupert Murdoch defended:
"On the racist thing, that caused a grilling. But Obama did make a very racist comment. Ahhh ... about, you know, blacks and whites and so on ... And um ... if you actually assess what Beck was talking about, he was right."

The Solution—
FucK Bill O'Reilly.
FucK Glenn Beck.
FucK Rupert Murdoch.
FucK Fox News.
FUCK RACISM.

*Fox fired O'Reilly after six sexual harassment suits against him were settled for $45 million.
**Beck departed Fox on 30 June 2011 after viewers and advertisers tired of his antics.

Becoming

After a restless night's sleep, I awoke this morning ready to drive, drive, drive.

My first destination: Meteor Crater, the site of an asteroid impact around 50,000 years ago—or about 40,000 years before Homo sapiens first migrated from Asia to the region.

"But an asteroid strike could not have occurred that long ago since the earth is less than 10,000 years old," a belief shared by 46 percent of Americans according to a 2012 Gallup poll.

Until 1543, a geocentric model of the universe prevailed as science. Today, 26 percent of Americans still believe that the sun revolves around the earth.

The Catholic Church, in 1633, convicted Galileo Galilei of heresy for advocating Copernicus' heliocentric model of the solar system. He spent the remainder of his life under house arrest.

> John Lennon had it wrong. God, in fact, is a concept that enables people to escape the truth. I shall say it again. God is a concept that enables people to escape the truth.
>
> Jesus said, *"The truth will set you free,"* unless you are Galileo of course.

Refusing to pay $15 to see the mile in diameter hole in the ground, I return to Interstate-40 East.

Magnificent clouds dance in unison across the sky until the Cholla Power Plant emerges and delivers clouds of coal combustion waste that emit carbon and sulfur dioxides into the sky, crocheting afghans of surging smog.

As I cross into New Mexico, the heavens rip open, and Navajo spirits dump divine tears of rain, furiously pelting the purlieu.

Visibility drops to thirty-feet for the next four hundred miles. But I welcome the cleansing power of the rain.

> Christianity does not encourage its adherents to seek spiritual cleansing through truth, only through repentance of *sin*.
>
> Christianity seeks definition through absolutes and dualities: right and wrong, good and evil, heaven and hell, God and Satan.
>
> Christianity, thereby, creates for its followers a black & white worldview, which wrongfully judges and condemns what lies outside its parochial realm of perception.
>
> But the world is not black & white. And one's perceptions should not be the sole gauge used in determining one's reality.

I used to live as if I were a surfer riding a wave: reacting to life's obstacles and challenges instead of overcoming life's obstacles and challenges by acting.

But I no longer want to *be* the surfer riding a wave.
I want, I long, to *be*come the wave.

Life is not *being*.
Life is *becoming*.

I *am* becoming.

A Truck Stop in Red Rock, New Mexico

another appears, a portly fellow, and
takes a seat in the booth next to mine.

like the others, he seems detached
(and tired) and void of any expression

of the slightest sign of happiness. we
exchange glances. my nod of approval

(and quick smile) goes unreturned.
suddenly, a pre-recorded public

address announcement interrupts
my lunch: *"shower customer 102,*

your shower is now ready.
please proceed to shower 14."

we, again, exchange glances.
my ensuing nod of approval

(and quick smile) also falls unreturned,
shifting my mood from amused

to horrified as our eyes in chorus
dart for the nearest exit. but upon

reflection, much to my surprise,
i surmised that not another soul

flinched, nor head turned, as each
blank face, unfazed by this rather

unusual declaration, calmly ate
from their plates (and sipped from

their cups) as if nothing
strange had transpired ...

save the portly fellow seated next
to me who promptly deserted his

meal (and paid his bill) before
swiftly departing the diner, smiling

and clutching a Hello Kitty
beach towel firmly in his hand.

Check Your Six

my fingers reek of raw leather,
as if i've been wearing baseball

batting gloves on both my hands
for the last three days. while this

possibility intrigues me, it seems
both impractical and highly unlikely

that i would engage in such a behavior.
i surmise a more logical explanation

for my freshly found odor: *The Lincoln's*
new, genuine pleather steering wheel

cover. the dual-lane highway is not the
most efficient mode of progress, but the

lack of traffic on US-56 along the Santa
Fe Trail through New Mexico, Oklahoma,

and Kansas allows me escape into a world
of translucent thought. cerulean skies cosset

careless cumulus clouds, cavorting with
Nephelai and creating an insurmountable

barrier between the firmament and
space-time continuum. despite my

repeated attempts to capture a floating
piece of cotton candy and soar away, the

wheels of *The Lincoln* remain glued to the
road and my body strapped to her front seat.

every fifty miles, or so, a small town
—a grain elevator and a water tower—

springs from the horizon. a community
of people must exist somewhere nearby,

but from the road, the prospect of thriving
life appears elusive. for the first time in

months, i am bewildered and insouciant,
void of emotion, and lack the vocabulary

to express my thoughts. we waste precious
time walking in circles, desperately grabbing

for what we think we *want*—that elusive
fixation forever dangling in front of us like

a hypnotist's gold-plated pocketwatch—
forgetting the entire time to grab a glance

and see that what we really *need* walks
patiently behind us with outstretched arms.

check your six before Time slips away.
check your six before it's too late.

)E-M-O-H(

                                                              Home—
        a place to rest your
head a pillow a warm
bed the backseat of a
car a rock under that bright
star seen through half-cracked front windows a dark waning
moon darting back and forth and forth and back across the
lagoon eyes envision curiosities coming and going with
        guitar in hand a dream:

        blue dirt visions of rose highways
painting a morphined sunbeam
carrying picasso
tripping in spite of everything
singing sounds (no more sounds) of engines
humming winds
whipping tiny blades of grass
growing green leaves
turning brown
falling to the ground prometheus unbound in a ten % solution
grifting spellbound sherlock
pilfering watson (no more)
waiting at home in motionless atrophy
lacking gravity
rebelling then floating
        (spontaneously)

        down algae laden alleys of
        down algae laden baggies of
        down algae laden valleys gandhi does dilly with e.e.

        progress stalls silence stonewalls poxy speedballs
sprawling A.W.O.L
calling nepal mauling
        (sol's cure-all)
                                        —nepal calls sol's cure-all

Ding-Dong! The Dick is Dead

amassed around a chiseled stone
ambushed mourners lament
the passing of the freshly fallen

from the necropolis wasteland
apostles of the cowboy prophet
picket his will of efficacious grace
onto the impiously unatoned

burdened by captured children
handpainted signs descend
like manna from Canaan
championing Christinsanity's
creed: "*God Hates Fags*"

absent in his hospice bed
the homophobe breathes his last
(gasp   gasp   gasp   gasp)
eluding immortality's grasp
his disbarred spirit condemned
into the lonesome hands of antipathy

Lonesome Langston

lonesome Langston
sits stag in the Jim Crow row
  entombed by his books

lonesome Langston
suffers sidelong in beautiful language
  enveloped by monochromatic
         monotheistic
         monosyllabic
               stockwhitefreestateleftbentlib
               er
               al
               think
               ing
               law
               rence
               minds

the train track leads Chicago way
the conductor pronounces the final boarding call
the steam trumpet noiselessly murmurs de rigueur counsel

"step back or step across the color line"
(*come forthwith Sandy in hues of laughter*)

and tell me when
you last saw
a black person
traipsing down
Mass Street?

GunpowderVodkaCowshit

townies linger in Lawrence
  (dropouts living in limbo)
skinny-jeaned hipster hucksters
  (lenses on their bridges
    pubes on their chins)
peddling direct trade round the clock coffee
pedaling east side brick side roads
  (hoping to catch a glimpse of Bill's ghost
     posing for a pic with a shotgun in his hand
   hoping to catch a glimpse of Bill's ghost
     posing for a pop with a shotofjunk in his hand)

but—
the pope of dope's defunct
the queer old man has split
the perfume of gunpowdervodkacowshit has vanished

  (and it's not coming back)

we surmised that—
the day they put a Chick-fil-A in Wescoe Hall
the day we finally accepted the Truth:
the River City ain't the Promised Land

she's a progressive's purgatory
deserted only by death or graduation

she's a scenester's Shangri-La
leased by lingering dropouts
  (townies living in limbo)
skinny-jeaned hipster hucksters
  (lenses on their bridges
    pubes on their chins)
peddling hopelessly pedaling
  (in wait of the queer old man's return)

Café Ephemera

In the Internet café,
hipsters come and go,
surfing wirelessly,
effortlessly adoring
their pieces, their Galaxies, their Motos.

Three screennames from which to choose,
three identities to assume.

He says, *"I'll have a café mocha, Grande.
Four shots, not three ... if there is room."*

The chat room seems a little fin today,
but Hipster A
needs to vent some rage,
needs to update his Twitter feed or Facebook page,
needs to post another page,
another post-modern blog by a nihilist sage,
exposing his life story for voyeurs to ingest,
kitsch for all to see
in the shallow sea
of DARPA technology,
sipping his coffee,
creating his own paparazzi,
photographs and selfies frozen in finality:
the eco-boomer's therapy,
the Google Generation's reality.

Gone.

The barista busses the vacant table,
preparing the space for another deck cronkite,
a paranoid prophet whose cowlicks and unshaven face
face the world with an i-Phone in one hand,
peeling an orange with the other.

"Brother," says Hipster B.
"Can you spare some change?
I need some kale for another Café au lait ...
Frank Einstein died today,"
I heard Madman say
while running away
from another day
of truth, light, and the American way.

In the Internet café,
hipsters come and go,
surfing aimlessly,
effortlessly adoring another shot of espresso.

Enter Hipster C:
"I'll move to Williamsburg someday.
Brooklyn that is ...
The North Side ...
Close to the L-Train."

Tragically unaware of the gentrification
and rising rents of this former bohemian domain,
platinum carrying scenesters
dominate this demographic of seduction
by high-rise construction
and waterfront rezoning
in the latest incarnation
of the SoHo-Effect of Manhattanization.

Artists flee to Philly,
which is the sixth borough we now know;
while in the Internet café,
hipsters come and go.

Goodbye

she sits solitarily
  studying anatomy
  sipping green tea
  silently knitting a sweater

her tousled hair
  angelic eyes
  sensual smile
    tempts me
    cheers me
    guides me
        like a lighthouse
        leading lost wayfarers
        seeking
          solace
        seeking
          shelter
        seeking
      someone, something
special

she glances at me again
  peers inquisitively
  penetrates my mind
  palpitates my heart

she stands to leave
  stops by my table
  slowly raises her hand, waves
  softly smiles, says

goodbye

Burning Jazz

jazz boils
squeaking
city streets
snare backbeat
jams trumpeting
head charts
learned by ear
without a single sheet
KC breathes
exhaling perfect notes
a bird flees its nest
   (gig bag fulla bebop
   blood pulsin' junk)
stealing away
a booming town's identity
immortalized at massey hall
brittle grafton jams
pocket backbeat
burning jazz
immured in plastic
under museum's cover
near 18th & Vine
city streets
speak

Giant Steps

he wanders into the wine bar
audaciously orders a martini dry
sounds the jazz trio's giant steps
reverberating off the tin ceiling

fans ruffling his benny hinn comb-over
coxcomb's not the typical barfly
on the wall street journal captured
under his arm wheeling and dealing

cell phone clipped to his kuiper belt
like captain kirk's communicator
velcroed to his khaki dockers and
lieutenant uhura's bluetooth headset

protruding from his miracle ear
muff diving sugar daddy suitor
who wins at last thanks not
to his charm but his red corvette

Taming Lions

suburban clone
of downtown pub
smells circus

poser hipsters in
flat-brimmed hats
cowboy hats

stocking caps
fedoras
compete in

three rings
singing
pop-corn culture dirges

masculinity compromised
by a pacifist *"faggot"*
an Iraq vet clowns antagonistically

walking a tightrope
between sanity
and madness

the ringmaster
choreographs
enlistees to the grave

Vanishing

deposited securely
in the zippered front pocket
of his sullied winter coat

thirty-eight dollars
(the day's
panhandling crop

harvested
on urban soil)
banks on asylum

from ne'er-do-wells
Ron absconds
on his red bicycle

exiting the transient stage
under florid snow flurries
his taillight twinkles

off and back on again
before vanishing
in the chasm of dolor

Snowflakes

snowflakes
remind me of
the time in sixth
grade when
dad and i
built a snowman
in the front yard only
to see it melt away like
the dreams of one's youth
slowing evaporating under the
intensity of the cold sun until
nothing remains but a
teardrop

Innocence: Gone

ice white pellets furiously
pelt transparent glass sheets,

embedding veracity.
wind chimes ring,

crooning insomniac dirges.
newspapers ricochet,

dancing in dissonant rhythm.
deaf ears languor,

slumbering in winter's hibernation.
purity erased by daylight's

cleansing blades. innocence: gone.
home, the dénouement.

)e-m-o-H(too: Sleepless Blues

                                        Home—
      a place to rest your
head a pillow a warm
sack the backseat of a
car the bitterseat of a
bus train or plane the sleeping
bag on the floor of a stranger's
apartment the inflatable
mattress on the floor of your parent's
office the hammock in your sister's
backyard the futon in your friend's
closet the unfamiliar bed of a
hotel motel or hostel the
tent pitched inches above high tide on a
beach under that lofty star a sunny waxing
moon envisions approaching fantasies loitering with
     guitar in hand a tune:

     i've got the space-heated attic
masqueradin' as my own crib air-matress on the
floorsleepin' middle of the night body achin' calf
crampin' eyes wide open hot as fuck dehydrated
     sleepless blues

     and one thing's for certain:
     all that lead me—*(w)here?*

Hiatus: of

words flow freely from fingertips to laptop keyboards transcribing
   thoughts of

reflections intimations without
   punctuation of

previously trapped deep in the
   recesses of

overdrive receptors sending swirling
   signals of

electrical current from shadowy
   chasms of

frozen spheres to void-less sweet
   stars of

eternal light
   apparitions of

forever endeavoring in accord with stringed dimensions born
   free of

defective (intelligently) designed intellectual
   idioms of

delicate and vicious descent upon
   screens of

illumination burning in harmony with media's etched
   contemplations of

vomited didactical dialects spewing
   diarrhea of

sages born and eyewitnesses
   unborn of

mentally digested constipated
   feelings of

current powering solared idyllic
   notions of

eastward motion in
   search of

oceans atlantic and cities secluded from dormant fault
   lines of

restrained puissance by scripture's sacred
   belts of

parochial new
   testaments of

white stripes selling chuck
   taylors of

innocent criminals capitulating to cadillac's
   cash of

modest mice floating on stars' satellite
   systems of

cake cutting slices into apple's
   core of

(no more)
   dreams of

lennon's imagination bombarding mainstreaming
   minds of

boomers' babies infantilized consumers shelled by nuclear
   discharges of

one party polity and plutocracy fashioning
   attitudes of

chasing caesar's dead presidents and huffing vitriolic
   granules of

soundbites kilobytes dust
   mites of

infected ratiocination inducing
   inhalation of

faculty and lungs filled to
   capacity of

digested regurgitated exhaled inertia superseding supplanted
   seeds of

sowers yore saving
   secrets of

straight-dope seekers searching for freely flowing transcribed
   words of

returned
   thoughts of

reflected congregating overcome
   banks of

crashing into bathed and waxed
   lincolns of

(breakingdentingsmashingcracking) taillight eternal raving into
   intimations of

free dimensions void-less apparitions forever in accord within
　imaginations of

projected possibilities on
　screens of

dreams from fingertips to laptop
　keyboards of

dreams to
　screens of

idyllic
　streams of
　consciousness of
　ideas of
　inspiration of

hypnotizing
　lines of

The Beat of Beats Passed

some write about
birds & trees & leaves & bees

and greet the day with innocent hymns
of backyard suburban sweet.

some write about
the street.

the beat
of beats passed.

the past realism
of a generation

in action
not without

imagination

but partaking
transcendent

surrealism
enabling

creation
in existentialism:

subjugation erased.

PRNDL: Anamnesis

Pages turn,
Recede, into the penumbra of anamnesis, yet
Neutral lines linger,
Departed from their homes,
Lost, between your hands and heart.

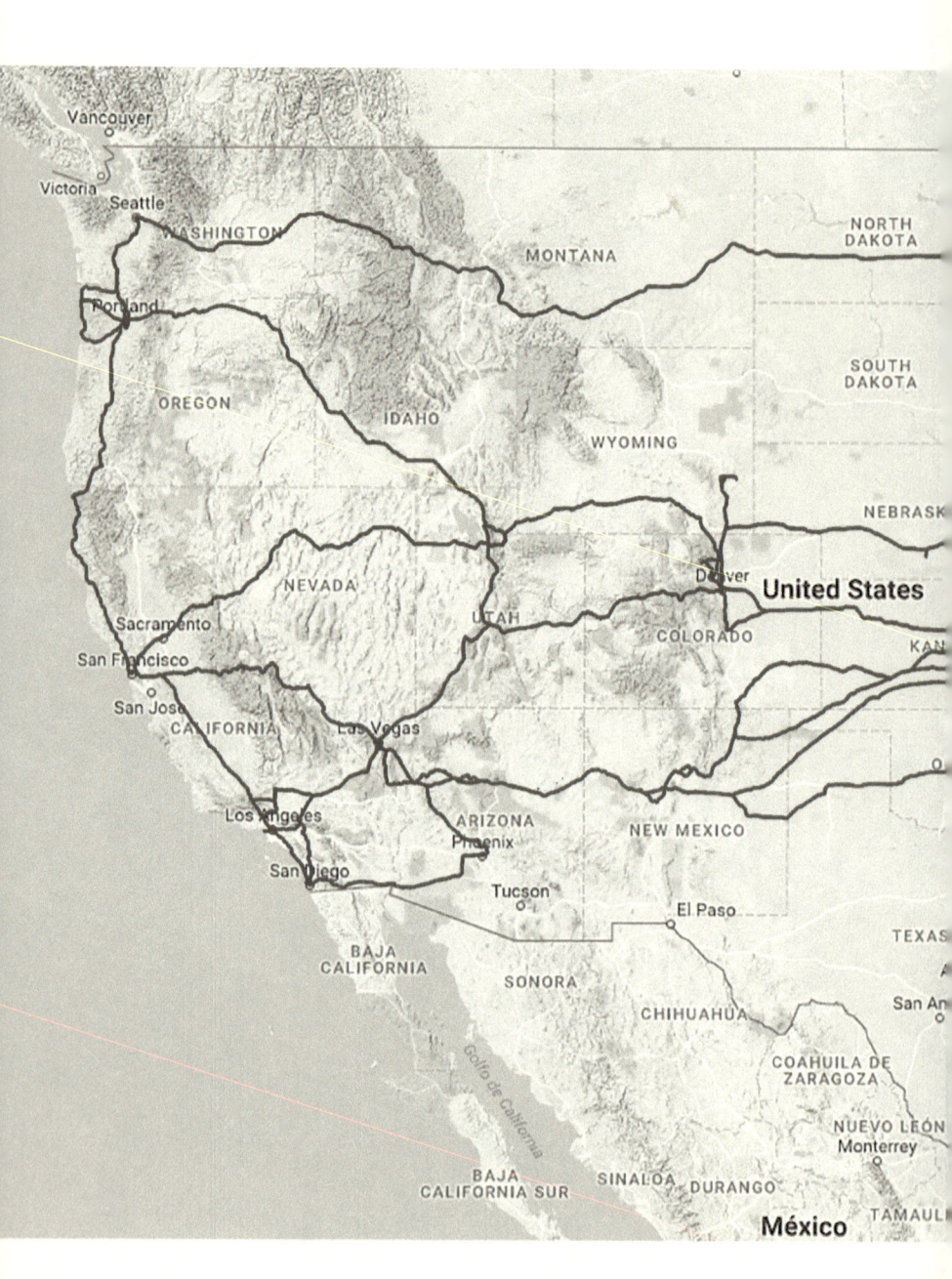

August 2010 – October 2015

ABOUT THE AUTHOR

j.d.tulloch is the founder and managing editor of 39 West Press. He has worked in broadcast radio and for the music management team of the late Godfather of Soul, James Brown.

www.ingramcontent.com/pod-product-compliance
Lightning Source LLC
Chambersburg PA
CBHW020616300426
44113CB00007B/668